A Scolar Press Facsimile

THE PHOENIX NEST

1593

Printed and published in Great Britain by
The Scolar Press Limited, Menston, Yorkshire
and 39 Great Russell Street, London WC1

This facsimile first published 1973

ISBN
0 85417 992 5
(Cloth)

ISBN
0 85417 993 3
(Paperback)

Introductory Note

With the notable exception of *Englands Helicon* (1600), this is the most attractive of the Elizabethan poetical miscellanies, well selected, edited and printed. The production of *The Phoenix Nest* was not, as was usually the case with such miscellanies, the commercial venture of a printer, but rather a literary and gentlemanly enterprise. We know nothing more of the compiler than the title page tells us, that 'R.S.' was a gentleman of the Inner Temple; and a similar well-bred reserve veils the identities of the various contributors to the volume, the poems being for the greater part unsigned, or at most given the author's initials. The good state of the texts provided for the collection, the almost entire omission of previously printed material and the association there is known to have been between some of the identifiable contributors, all suggest that R. S. put together in *The Phoenix Nest* a selection of work by his friends, to whose original texts he had access. The Phoenix of the title was clearly Sidney. His death in 1586 is lamented in three elegies which stand at the head of the volume (if we discount the prose piece on the Earl of Leicester, which the pagination makes clear was added at a late stage to fill an unexpected gap); and perhaps it was with the publication of *Astrophel and Stella* in 1591, that in a sense the Phoenix arose from the ashes. It seems not unlikely, at any rate, that the publication of Sidney's sonnets inspired R. S. to assemble *The Phoenix Nest*.

The miscellany caught the new poetic manner, which Sidney heralded and inspired, although there is a good deal of drab matter in the older style, especially in the first part of the volume, to sig. G2. The most frequently represented of the identifiable contributors and the most significant contributor to the new poetic tone was Thomas Lodge, but other well-known names were concealed behind various of the sets of initials, Nicholas Breton, George Peele, and Edward de Vere, Earl of Oxford.

Oddly, the single edition of *The Phoenix Nest* suggests that it was not very popular, unless we are to suppose that much use wore away subsequent editions. The one edition was extremely well printed by John Jackson, and is reproduced here from a fine copy, by permission of the Curators of the Bodleian Library (*shelfmark:* Mal 287).

References: STC 21516; *The Phoenix Nest, 1593*, edit. by H. E. Rollins, 1931.

D. E. L. CRANE

THE
PHOENIX
NEST.

Built vp with the moſt rare
and refined workes of Noble
men, woorthy Knights, gallant
Gentlemen, Maſters of
Arts, and braue
Schollers.

Full of varietie, excellent inuen-
tion, and ſingular
delight.

Neuer before this time publiſhed.

Set foorth by R. S. of
the Inner Temple
Gentleman.

Imprinted at London, by
Iohn Iackſon.

1 5 9 3

This Booke containeth thefe 14. moſt
ſpeciall and woorthie
workes.

1   The dead mans Right.

2   An excellent Elegie, with two ſpeciall
      Epitaphes vpon the death of ſir Philip
      Sydney,   pag.1.

3   The praiſe of Chaſtitie,   12

4   A Dialogue betweene Conſtancie and
      Inconſtancie,   16

5   A Garden plot,   21

6   A Dream of Ladies & their Riddles, 23

7   The Cheſſe play,   28

8   Another rare Dreame,   31

9   An excellent Paſſion,   63

10   A notable deſcription of the World, 77

11   A Counterloue,   80

12   A deſcription of Loue,   90

13   A deſcription of Iealouſie, 91

14   The praiſe of Virginitie, 93

With other excellent and rare
Ditties.

A 2

A Preface to the Reader vpon
the dead mans
Right.

 Write not(gentle Rea-
der) to flatter, for the
dead are not vainglo-
rious: nor to gain,they
reward not trauels: for
pride leſſe, they are o-
ther mens vertues not
mine owne that I pub-
liſh : for malice leaſt of all, bicauſe I ſee how
ill it becomes them to whom I write. But I
write to admoniſh, and (if it might be) to a-
mend vile and enuious toongs: if not, I ſeeke
no other hire nor glorie than the ſatisfa-
ction of mine owne conſcience,
by diſcharging the dutie of
a Chriſtian. So fare
you well.

The dead mans Right.

Written vpon the death of the Right Honorable the
Earle of Leiceſter.

T is not vnknowne how wicked Libel-
lors haue moſt odiouſlye ſought the
ſlander of our wiſe, graue, and Hono-
rable ſuperiours : diuulging defamato-
rie Libels, ſo full of immodeſt railings
and audacious lies, as no indifferent
Reader but may eaſily diſcouer their
enuie, and iudge of the veritie : The
Authors whereof, though in the quali-
tie of their offence (tending wholie to ſedition) they haue
woorthily deſerued death, yet the ſubſtance of their Pam-
phlets haue not merited anſwere.

For want whereof ſome as euill affected as themſelues, to
whoſe hands moſtly ſuch bookes haue come, are flattered
with a poore aduantage, imputing the wiſe and ſilent diſge-
ſting of ſuch inhoneſt and ſcurilous cartels to their guil-
tineſſe : when (ſimple as they are) who is elſe ſo fooliſh as
knoweth not if all diuulged were true, how eaſily Authori-
tie might excuſe them, hauing pens and Preſſes at comman-
dement, and power to patronize : Much more when ſo vn-
true as themſelues aſhamed of their falſhoodes, dare not
auouch them vnder their owne names being without reach
and feare of Authoritie.

Amongſt others, whoſe Honors theſe intemperate railors
haue ſought to ſcandalize, none haue more vildly bin ſlan-
dered than the late deceaſed Earle, the godly, loiall, wiſe, and
graue Earle of Leiceſter: Againſt whom (void of all iuſt touch
of

of diſhonor) they forged millions of impieties, abuſing the
people by their diuieliſh fictions , and wicked wreſting of his
actions, all to bring his vertues & perſon in popular hatred.

Which though he during his life meekely bare as a man
vntouched, without publiſhing defence of his innocencie.
Yet becauſe the toongs of men irritated to enuie by the in-
ſtruments of thoſe libellors, being without feare of control-
ment, ſith his death are become ouer ſcandalous and at too
much libertie. It ſhall not be amiſſe to perſwade more mo-
deſtie and pietie of ſpeech.

And for as much as I perceiue the greateſt and moſt gene-
rall obiection they haue to blemiſh his honor, is but an opi-
nion of his ambition and aſpiring minde , wherewith the
capitall and cardinall Libellor of them all hath cunninglie
infected the ignorant that knew not the ſtate of his honors:
Let vs ſee how he may iuſtly be touched.

Did he euer aſſume vnto himſelfe anie vaine or vnlawfull
tytle, or was vnſatiate of rule ? Did he purchaſe his honors
otherwiſe than by his vertues, or were they ſo extraordina-
rie, as nowe or in times paſt they haue not beene equaled in
others inferior vnto him in condition of birth, and more in
deſart ? If not ? I maruell the father of this peſtilent inuenti-
on bluſh not as red as his cap , and his children be not aſha-
med of his falſehood.

Admit this woorthie Earles and our moſt gratious Soue-
reigne who wiſely iudged of his vertues, and worthily rewar-
ded his loialtie and paines, did honor him with titles aboue
others of his time: (in humble and ſeemely ſort, I ſpeake it
without compariſon) who euery way was more fit for the
dignitie he bare, and more complet to accompliſh them :
whereof the Libellor could not be ignoraunt , but that too
much yeelding to his malice, he ſought to ſlaunder this nota-
ble teſtimonie of his Excellencie.

Such rather woulde I iudge ambitious, as for promoti-
ons whether Eccleſiaſticall or Temporall, hauing once con-
ceiued a hope of greatneſſe, without regard of conſcience or
Countrie , with voluntarie hazarde of all things purſue the
ſame,

ſame, by ſhamefull, traiterous, and vngodlie meanes, exaſpe-
rating their naturall Prince and ſuperiour Magiſtrates by re-
bellious and ſeditious Libels. Theſe be the true tokens of an
aſpiring minde, whoſe nature is to hinder by malice, where it
can not hurt by power.

But leauing further purſute of their malice, I will remem-
ber this Earles woorthineſſe. For the firſt and principall ver-
tue of his vertues, his Religion, it ſhall be needleſſe to ſpeake
much, ſith all Chriſtendome knows he profeſſed one Faith,
and worſhipped one onely God, whom he ſerued in vpright-
nes of life, and defended with hazard thereof in armes and
action againſt his enimies. How he ſuccoured and relieued
diſtreſſed members of the Church, I leaue to thoſe that haue
made proofe, who ought in dutie to make relation thereof.

Next I thinke there is none that will, dare, or can impeach
his loialtie, either in fact or faith, ſufficiently teſtified by hir
Maieſties gratious loue to whom that belonged, as alſo by
his dutifull and carefull ſeruice vnto hir. So as further narra-
tion thereof ſhall not neede.

His wiſedome by the grauitie of his place, the cauſes he
managed, and the cariage of his perſon, is approoued not
onely vnto vs, but to moſt nations of the world.

Laſtlie of his valour and affection to his Countries peace,
no honeſt minde but is ſatisfied: whereof what greater teſti-
monie can we require than the trauels his aged bodie vnder-
tooke, and dangers the ſame was ſubiect vnto in the warres
of the Low Countries, where he voluntarily offered his per-
ſon in combate againſt the deuoted enimies of this ſtate and
hir Maieſtie. Leauing his Wife, poſſeſſions, and home, not
regarding his ſafetie, riches, and eaſe, in reſpect of the godly,
honourable, and louing care he bare the common quiet.

All which the vngratefull Malecontents of this time, on
whome any thing is ill beſtowed (much more the trauels of
ſo memorable a Noble) ſpared not to reproch : Hyring the
toongs of runawaies and roges, ſuch as neither feare God
nor the diuell, or are woorth a home, to proclaime hatefull
and enuious lies againſt him, in alehouſes, faires, markets,

and

and ſuch aſſemblies.

At whoſe returne when his dealings were truely diſcuſſed, and truth ouercame their ſlanders, this was the refuge of their whiſpering malice: His greatneſſe and ſmooth toong (ſaie they) beares it awaie: as if Honor once loſt in act, could be hidden by greatnes, or recouered by grace and eloquence of ſpeech. Both which taken away by his happie death, and our vnhappie loſſe, he is ſithence more cleared than before.

Maruell not then at their enuie, ſith, *Virtutis comes inuidia*, but deteſt the enuious, that thus blaſpheme vertues, whom (for mine owne part) as I ſee meaſure their rage, ſo will I iudge of their affection to the ſtate: for vndoubtedly none but the diſcontented with the time, or ſuch as he hath iuſtlie puniſhed for their lewdneſſe, will thus calumniouſlie interpret his proceedings.

If I meant to write a diſcourſe of this Earles life, or an Apologie in his defence, I would proceede more orderly in repetition of his vertues, and more effectually in anſwere of their poiſoned Libels: But as mine intent at firſt was onelie to admoniſh looſe toongs (ſuch as mine eares haue glowed to heare of) and forewarne the ouer credulous that are eaſily abuſed, hauing finiſhed my purpoſe, if it effects amendment, I ſhall be glad, if not, their ſhames be on their owne heads.

Beſeeching God this Realme feele not the want of him alreadie dead, and greater iudgements inſue for our vnthankfulneſſe.

Leicester he liu'd, of all the world admir'd,
Not as a man, though he in ſhape exceld:
But as a God, whoſe heauenlie wit inſpir'd,
Wrought hie effects, yet vertues courſes held,
His wiſdome honored his Countries name,
His valure was the vangard of the ſame.

An Elegie, or friends paſſion, for
his Aſtrophill.

Written vpon the death of the right Honorable ſir Philip
Sidney knight, Lord gouernor of
Fluſhing.

AS then, no winde at all there blew,
No ſwelling cloude, accloid the aire,
The ſkie, like glaſſe of watchet hew,
Reflected Phœbus golden haire,
  The garniſht tree, no pendant ſtird,
  No voice was heard of any bird.

There might you ſee the burly Beare,
The Lion king, the Elephant,
The maiden Vnicorne was there,
So was Acteons horned plant,
  And what of wilde or tame are found,
  Were coucht in order on the ground.

Alcides ſpeckled poplar tree,
The palme that Monarchs doe obtaine,
With Loue iuice ſtaind the mulberie,
The fruit that dewes the Poets braine,
  And Phillis philbert there away,
  Comparde with mirtle and the bay.

The tree that coffins doth adorne,
With ſtately height threatning the ſkie,
And for the bed of Loue forlorne,
The blacke and dolefull Ebonie,
  All in a circle compaſt were,
  Like to an Amphitheater.

Vpon the branches of thoſe trees,
The airie winged people ſat,
  B   Diſtinguiſhed

Diſtinguiſhed in od degrees,
One ſort in this, another that,
    Here Philomell, that knowes full well,
    What force and wit in loue doth dwell.

The skie bred Egle roiall bird,
Percht there vpon an oke aboue,
The Turtle by him neuer ſtird,
Example of immortall loue.
    The ſwan that ſings about to dy,
    Leauing Meander ſtood thereby.

And that which was of woonder moſt,
The Phœnix left ſweete Arabie :
And on a Cædar in this coaſt,
Built vp hir tombe of ſpicerie,
    As I coniecture by the ſame,
    Preparde to take hir dying flame.

In midſt and center of this plot,
I ſaw one groueling on the graſſe :
A man or ſtone, I knew not that,
No ſtone, of man the figure was,
    And yet I could not count him one,
    More than the image made of ſtone.

At length I might perceiue him reare
His bodie on his elbow end :
Earthly and pale with gaſtly cheare,
Vpon his knees he vpward tend,
    Seeming like one in vncouth ſtound,
    To be aſcending out the ground.

A greeuous ſigh foorthwith he throwes,
As might haue torne the vitall ſtrings,
Then downe his cheekes the teares ſo flowes,
As doth the ſtreame of many ſprings.

                                    So

So thunder rends the cloud in twaine,
And makes a paſſage for the raine.

Incontinent with trembling ſound,
He wofully gan to complaine,
Such were the accents as might wound,
And teare a diamond rocke in twaine,
　　After his throbs did ſomwhat ſtay,
　　Thus heauily he gan to ſay.

O ſunne (ſaid he) ſeeing the ſunne,
On wretched me why doſt thou ſhine,
My ſtar is falne, my comfort done,
Out is the apple of my eine,
　　Shine vpon thoſe poſſeſſe delight,
　　And let me liue in endleſſe might.

O griefe that lieſt vpon my ſoule,
As heauie as a mount of lead,
The remnant of my life controll,
Conſort me quickly with the dead,
　　Halfe of this hart, this ſprite and will,
　　Di'de in the breſt of Aſtrophill.

And you compaſſionate of my wo,
Gentle birds, beaſts and ſhadie trees,
I am aſſurde ye long to kno,
What be the ſorrowes me agreeu's,
　　Liſten ye then to that inſu'th,
　　And heare a tale of teares and ruthe.

You knew, who knew not Aſtrophill,
(That I ſhould liue to ſay I knew,
And haue not in poſſeſſion ſtill)
Things knowne permit me to renew,
　　Of him you know his merit ſuch,
　　I cannot ſay, you heare too much.

Within these woods of Arcadie,
He cheefe delight and pleasure tooke,
And on the mountaine Parthenie,
Vpon the chrystall liquid brooke,
 The Muses met him eu'ry day,
 That taught him sing,to write,and say.

When he descended downe the mount,
His personage seemed most diuine,
A thousand graces one might count,
Vpon his louely cheerefull eine,
 To heare him speake and sweetely smile,
 You were in Paradise the while.

A sweete attractiue kinde of grace,
A full assurance giuen by lookes,
Continuall comfort in a face,
The lineaments of Gospell books,
 I trowe that countenance cannot lie,
 Whose thoughts are legible in the eie.

Was neuer eie,did see that face,
Was neuer eare,did heare that tong,
Was neuer minde,did minde his grace,
That euer thought the trauell long,
 But eies,and eares,and eu'ry thought,
 Were with his sweete perfections caught.

O God,that such a woorthy man,
In whom so rare desarts did raigne,
Desired thus,must leaue vs than,
And we to wish for him in vaine,
 O could the stars that bred that wit,
 In force no longer fixed sit.

Then being fild with learned dew,
The Muses willed him to loue,

          That

That inſtrument can aptly ſhew,
How finely our conceits will moue,
   As Bacchus opes diſſembled harts,
   So loue ſets out our better parts.

Stella, a Nymph within this wood,
Moſt rare and rich of heauenly blis,
The higheſt in his fancie ſtood,
And ſhe could well demerite this,
   Tis likely they acquainted ſoone,
   He was a Sun, and ſhe a Moone.

Our Aſtrophill did Stella loue,
O Stella vaunt of Aſtrophill,
Albeit thy graces gods may moue,
Where wilt thou finde an Aſtrophill,
   The roſe and lillie haue their prime,
   And ſo hath beautie but a time.

Although thy beautie doe exceede,
In common ſight of eu'ry eie,
Yet in his Poeſies when we reede,
It is apparant more thereby,
   He that hath loue and iudgement too,
   Sees more than any other doe.

Then Aſtrophill hath honord thee,
For when thy bodie is extinct,
Thy graces ſhall eternall be,
And liue by vertue of his inke,
   For by his verſes he doth giue,
   To ſhort liude beautie aye to liue.

Aboue all others this is hee,
Which erſt approoued in his ſong,
That loue and honor might agree,
And that pure loue will doe no wrong,

                                Sweete

Sweete ſaints it is no ſinne nor blame,
To loue a man of vertuous name.

Did neuer loue ſo ſweetly breath
In any mortall breſt before,
Did neuer muſe inſpire beneath,
A Poets braine with finer ſtore:
  He wrote of loue with high conceit,
  And beautie reard aboue hir height.

Then Pallas afterward attyrde,
Our Aſtrophill with hir deuice,
Whom in his armor heauen admyrde,
As of the nation of the skies,
  He ſparkled in his armes afarrs,
  As he were dight with fierie ſtarrs.

The blaze whereof when Mars beheld,
(An enuious eie doth ſee afar)
Such maieſtie (quoth he) is ſeeld,
Such maieſtie my mart may mar,
  Perhaps this may a ſuter be,
  To ſet Mars by his deitie.

In this ſurmize he made with ſpeede,
An iron cane wherein he put,
The thunder that in cloudes do breede,
The flame and bolt togither ſhut.
  With priuie force burſt out againe,
  And ſo our Aſtrophill was ſlaine.

This word (was ſlaine) ſtraightway did moue,
And natures inward life ſtrings twitch,
The skie immediately aboue,
Was dimd with hideous clouds of pitch,
  The wraſtling winds from out the ground,
  Fild all the aire with ratling ſound.

The

The bending trees expreſt a grone,
And ſigh'd the ſorow of his fall,
The forreſt beaſts made ruthfull mone,
The birds did tune their mourning call,
    And Philomell for Aſtrophill,
    Vnto hir notes annext a phill.

The turtle doue with tunes of ruthe,
Shewd feeling paſſion of his death,
Me thought ſhe ſaid I tell thee truthe,
Was neuer he that drew in breath,
    Vnto his loue more truſtie found,
    Than he for whom our griefs abound.

The ſwan that was in preſence heere,
Began his funerall dirge to ſing,
Good things (quoth he) may ſcarce appeere,
But paſſe away with ſpeedie wing.
    This mortall life as death is tride,
    And death giues life, and ſo he di'de.

The generall ſorrow that was made,
Among the creatures of kinde,
Fired the Phœnix where ſhe laide,
Hir aſhes flying with the winde,
    So as I might with reaſon ſee,
    That ſuch a Phœnix nere ſhould bee.

Haply the cinders driuen about,
May breede an offspring neere that kinde,
But hardly a peere to that I doubt,
It cannot ſinke into my minde,
    That vnder branches ere can bee,
    Of worth and value as the tree.

The Egle markt with pearcing ſight,
The mournfull habite of the place,

                           And

And parted thence with mounting flight,
To ſignifie to Ioue the caſe,
What ſorow nature doth ſuſtaine,
For Aſtrophill by enuie ſlaine.

And while I followed with mine eie,
The flight the Egle vpward tooke,
All things did vaniſh by and by,
And diſappeered from my looke,
The trees,beaſts,birds,and groue was gone,
So was the friend that made this mone.

This ſpectacle had firmely wrought,
A deepe compaſſion in my ſpright,
My molting hart iſſude me thought,
In ſtreames foorth at mine eies aright,
And heere my pen is forſt to ſhrinke,
My teares diſcollors ſo mine inke.

An Epitaph vpon the right Honorable
ſir Philip Sidney knight : Lord
gouernor of Fluſhing.

TO praiſe thy life,or waile thy woorthie death,
And want thy wit,thy wit high,pure,diuine,
Is far beyond the powre of mortall line,
Nor any one hath worth that draweth breath.

Yet rich in zeale,though poore in learnings lore,
And friendly care obſcurde in ſecret breſt,
And loue that enuie in thy life ſuppreſt,
Thy deere life done, and death hath doubled more.

And I, that in thy time and liuing ſtate,
Did onely praiſe thy vertues in my thought,
As one that ſeeld the riſing ſunne hath ſought,
With words and teares now waile thy timeleſſe fate.

Drawne

Drawne was thy race, aright from princely line,
Nor leffe than fuch, (by gifts that nature gaue,
The common mother that all creatures haue,)
Doth vertue fhew, and princely linage fhine.

A king gaue thee thy name, a kingly minde,
That God thee gaue, who found it now too deere
For this bafe world, and hath refumde it neere,
To fit in skies, and fort with powres diuine.

Kent thy birth daies, and Oxford held thy youth,
The heauens made hafte, & ftaide nor yeeres, nor time,
The fruits of age grew ripe in thy firft prime,
Thy will, thy words ; thy words, the feales of truth.

Great gifts and wifedome rare imploide thee thence,
To treat from kings, with thofe more great than kings,
Such hope men had to lay the higheft things,
On thy wife youth, to be tranfported hence.

Whence to fharpe wars fweete honor did thee call,
Thy countries loue, religion, and thy friends :
Of woorthy men, the marks, the liues and ends,
And her defence, for whom we labor all.

There didft thou vanquifh fhame and tedious age,
Griefe, forow, ficknes, and bafe fortunes might :
Thy rifing day, faw neuer wofull night,
But paft with praife, from of this worldly ftage.

Backe to the campe, by thee that day was brought,
Firft thine owne death, and after thy long fame ;
Teares to the foldiers, the proud Caftilians fhame ;
Vertue expreft, and honor truly taught.

What hath he loft, that fuch great grace hath woon,
Yoong yeeres, for endles yeeres, and hope vnfure,

C   Of

Of fortunes gifts,for wealth that ſtill ſhall dure,
Oh happie race with ſo great praiſes run.

England doth hold thy lims that bred the ſame,
Flaunders thy valure where it laſt was tried,
The Campe thy ſorow where thy bodie died,
Thy friends,thy want;the world, thy vertues fame.

Nations thy wit,our mindes lay vp thy loue,
Letters thy learning,thy loſſe,yeeres long to come,
In worthy harts ſorow hath made thy tombe,
Thy ſoule and ſpright enrich the heauens aboue.

Thy liberall hart imbalmd in gratefull teares.
Yoong ſighes,ſweete ſighes,ſage ſighes,bewaile thy **fall**,
Enuie hir ſting,and ſpite hath left hir gall,
Malice hir ſelfe,a mourning garment weares.

That day their Haniball died,our Scipio fell,
Scipio,Cicero,and Petrarch of our time,
Whoſe vertues wounded by my woorthles rime,
Let Angels ſpeake,and heauens thy praiſes tell.

Another of the ſame.

Excellently written by a moſt woorthy Gentleman.

S Ilence augmenteth griefe,writing encreaſeth rage,   (age,
  Stald are my thoughts,which lou'd,& loſt,the wonder of our
Yet quickned now with fire,though dead with froſt ere now,
Enrag'de I write, I know not what:dead,quick,I know not how.

Hard harted mindes relent,and rigors teares abound,
And enuie ſtrangely rues his end,in whom no fault ſhe found,
Knowledge hir light hath loſt,valor hath ſlaine hir knight,
Sidney is dead,dead is my friend,dead is the worlds delight.

Place penſiue wailes his fall,whoſe preſence was hir pride,
Time crieth out,my ebbe is come : his life was my ſpring tide,
                                                 Fame

Fame mournes in that ſhe loſt,the ground of hir reports,
Ech liuing wight laments his lacke,and all in ſundry ſorts.

He was(wo worth that word)to ech well thinking minde,
A ſpotleſſe friend,a matchles man,whoſe vertue euer ſhinde,
Declaring in his thoughts,his life,and that he writ,
Higheſt conceits,longeſt foreſights,and deepeſt works of wit.

He onely like himſelfe,was ſecond vnto none,
Whoſe deth(though life)we rue,& wrong,& al in vain do mone,
Their loſſe,not him waile they,that fill the world with cries,
Death ſlue not him,but he made death his ladder to the skies.

Now ſinke of ſorow I,who liue,the more the wrong,
Who wiſhing death,whom deth denies,whoſe thred is al to long,
Who tied to wretched life,who lookes for no reliefe,
Muſt ſpend my euer dying daies,in neuer ending griefe.

Harts eaſe and onely I, like parables run on,
Whoſe equall length,keepe equall bredth, & neuer meet in one,
Yet for not wronging him,my thoughts,my ſorowes cell,
Shall not run out,though leake they will,for liking him ſo well.

Farewell to you my hopes,my wonted waking dreames,
Farewell ſomtimes enioied ioy,eclipſed are thy beames,
Farewell ſelfe pleaſing thoughts,which quietnes brings foorth,
And farewel friendſhips ſacred league, vniting minds of woorth.

And farewell mery hart,the gift of guiltles mindes,
And all ſports,which for liues reſtore,varietie aſſignes,
Let all that ſweete is,voide ? in me no mirth may dwell,
Philip,the cauſe of all this woe,my liues content farewell.

Now rime,the ſonne of rage,which art no kin to skill,   (kill,
And endles griefe, which deads my life, yet knowes not how to
Go ſeeke that haples tombe,which if ye hap to finde,
Salute the ſtones,that keepe the lims,that held ſo good a minde.

The praise of Chastitie.

Wherein is set foorth by way of comparison, how great
is the conquest ouer our affections,
by G. P. Master of
Arts.

THe noble Romans whilom woonted were,
 For triumph of their conquered enimies,
 The wreathes of Laurell, and of Palme to weare,
In honor of their famous victories,

And so in robes of gold, and purple dight,
 Like bodies shrinde, in seates of Iuorie,
Their names renowmde for happines in fight,
 They beare the guerdon of their chiualrie.

The valiant Greekes, for sacke of Priams towne,
 A worke of manhood, matcht with policie,
Haue fild the world with bookes of their renowne,
 As much as erst the Romane emperie.

The Phrygian knights, that in the house of fame,
 Haue shining armes of endles memorie,
By hot and fierce repulse did win the same,
 Though Helens rape, hurt Paris progenie.

Thus strength hath guerdon, by the worlds award,
 So praise we birth, and high nobilitie,
If then the minde, and bodie reape reward,
 For natures dowre, conferred liberally.

Presse then for praise, vnto the highest roome,
 That art the highest of the gifts of heauen,
More beautifull by wisdomes sacred doome,
 Than Sol himselfe, amid the Planets seauen.

          Queene

Queene of content,and temperate deſires,
    Choice nurſe of health,thy name hight Chaſtitie,
A ſoueraigne powre to quench ſuch climing fires,
    As choake the minde,with ſmoke of infamie.

Champion at armes,re'ncounter with thy foe,
    An enimie foule,and fearfull to behold,
If then ſtout captaines haue bene honor'd ſo,
    Their names in bookes of memorie enrold,

For puiſſant ſtrength : ye Romane peeres retire,
    And Greeks giue ground,more honor there is woon,
With chaſte rebukes to temper thy deſire,
    Than glory gaind the world to ouer run.

Than fierce Achilles got,by Hectors ſpoyle,
    Than erſt the mightie prince of Macedon,
King Philips impe,that put his foes to ſoyle,
    And wiſht more worlds to hold him plaie than one.

Beleeue me to contend 'gainſt armies royall,
    To tame wilde Panthers but by ſtrength of hand,
To praiſe the triumph,not ſo ſpeciall,
    As ticing pleaſures charmes for to withſtand.

And for me liſt compare with men of war,
    For honor of the field,I dare maintaine,
This victory exceedeth that as far,
    As Phœbus chariot Vulcans forge doth ſtaine.

Both noble,and triumphant in their kindes,
    And matter woorthie queene Remembrance pen,
But that that tangles both our thoughts and mindes,
    To maſter that,is more than ouer men,

To make thy triumph. Sith to ſtrength alone,
    Of body it belongs,to bruze or wound,
                     But

But raging thoughts, to quell, or few, or none,
   Saue vertues imps, are able champions found.

Or thoſe whom Ioue hath lou'd ? or noble of birth,
   So ſtrong Alcydes, Ioues vnconquered ſon,
Did lift Achelous bodie from the earth,
   To ſhew what deeds by vertues ſtrength are don.

So him he foild, and put to ſudden flight,
   By aime of wit, the foule Stimphalides ?
And while we ſay he maſtered men by might,
   Behold in perſon of this Hercules.

It liketh me to figure Chaſtitie,
   His labor like that foule vncleane deſire,
That vnder guide of tickling fantaſie,   (fire.
   Would mar the minde, through pleaſures ſcorching

And who hath ſeene a faire alluring face,
   A luſtie girle, yclad in queint aray,
Whoſe daintie hand, makes muſicke with hir lace,
   And tempts thy thoughts, and ſteales thy ſenſe away.

Whoſe ticing haire, like nets of golden wyre,
   Enchaine thy hart, whoſe gate and voice diuine,
Enflame thy blood, and kindle thy deſire,
   Whoſe features wrap and dazle humaine eine.

Who hath beheld faire Venus in hir pride,
   Of nakednes all Alablaſter white,
In Iuorie bed, ſtrait laid by Mars his ſide,
   And hath not bin enchanted with the ſight,

To wiſh, to dallie, and to offer game,
   To coy, to court, & cætera to doe :
(Forgiue me Chaſtnes if in termes of ſhame,
   To thy renowne, I paint what longs thereto)

                           Who

Who hath not liu'd,and yet hath ſeene I ſay,
   That might offend chaſte hearers to endure,
Who hath bene haled on,to touch,and play,
   And yet not ſtowpt to pleaſures wanton lure.

Crowne him with laurell,for his victorie,
   Clad him in purple,and in ſcarlet die?
Enroll his name in bookes of memorie,
   Ne let the honor of his conqueſt die.

More roiall in his triumph, than the man,
   Whom tygres drew in coach of burniſht golde,
In whom the Roman Monarchie began,
   Whoſe works of worth,no wit hath erſt controlde.

Elyſium be his walke,high heauen his ſhrine,
   His drinke,ſweete Nectar,and Ambroſia,
The foode that makes immortall and diuine,
   Be his to taſte,to make him liue for ay:

And that I may in briefe deſcribe his due,
   What laſting honor vertues guerdon is,
So much and more his iuſt deſart purſue,
   Sith his deſart awards it to be his.

LENVOY.

To thee in honor of whoſe gouernment,
   Entitled is this praiſe of Chaſtitie,
My gentle friend,theſe haſtie lines are ment,
   So flowreth vertue like the laurell tree,
   Immortall greene,that euere eie may ſee,
      And well was Daphne turnd into the bay,
      Whoſe chaſtnes triumphes,growes, & liues for ay.

An

An excellent Dialogue betweene Conſtancie
and Inconſtancie, as it was by ſpeech preſented
to hir Maieſtie, in the laſt Progreſſe at
ſir Henrie Leighes houſe.

Con-
ſtan-
cie.

Oſt excellent: ſhall I ſay Lady, or Goddeſſe ? whom I ſhould enuie to be but a Lady, and can not denie to haue the power of a Goddeſſe ? vouchſafe to accept the humble thankfulnes of vs lately diſtreſſed Ladies, the pride of whoſe wits was iuſtly puniſhed with the inconſtancie of our wits; whereby we were caried to delight, as in nothing more than to loue, ſo in nothing ſo much as to change louers; which puniſhment, though it were onely due to our diſcents, yet did it light moſt heauily vpon thoſe knights, who following vs with the heate of their affection, had neither grace to get vs, nor power to leaue vs. Now ſince by that more than moꝛtall power of your more than humane wiſedome, the enchanted tables are read, and both they and we releaſed, let vs be puniſhed with more than inconſtancie, if we faile either to loue conſtantly, or to alienize your memorie.

Inconſtancie. Not to be thankfull to ſo great a perſon, for ſo great a benefite, might argue as little iudgement, as ill nature : and therefore though it be my place to ſpeake after you, I will ſtriue in thankfulnes to go before you, but yet rather for my libertie, bicauſe I may be as I liſt, than for any minde I haue to be moꝛe conſtant than I was.

Conſt. If you haue no minde to be conſtant, what is the benefit of your deliuerance ?

Inconſt.

Inconſt. As I tolde you before, my libertie,which I loue
better than my ſelfe; for though I loue inconſtancie
as my ſelfe, and had as leeue not be, as not be vn-
conſtant ; yet can I not but hate that which I loue;
but when I am enforced vnto it:and(by your leaue)
as daintie as you make of the matter, I am perſwa-
ded that you would euen hate your ſelfe , if you
were but wedded vnto your ſelfe.

Conſt. Selfeloue is not the loue that we talke of, but ra-
ther the kinde of knitting of two harts in one , of
which ſort if you had a faithfull louer, what ſhoulde
you looſe by being faithfull vnto him ?

Inconſt. More than you ſhall get by being ſo.

Conſt. I ſeeke nothing but him to whom I am conſtant.

Inconſt. And euen him ſhall you looſe by being conſtant.

Conſt. What reaſon haue you for that ?

Inconſt. No other reaſon than that which is drawn from
the common places of loue, which is for the moſt
part,reaſon beyond reaſon.

Conſt. You may rather call it reaſon without reaſon; if
they conclude that loue and faith , the more they
haue,the leſſe they ſhall finde.

Inconſt. Will you beleeue your owne experience ?

Conſt. Farre beyond your reaſon.

Inconſt. Haue you not then found amongſt your louers,
that they would flie you, if you do but follow them,
and follow you moſt, when you do moſt flie them ?

Conſt. I graunt I haue found it too true in ſome, but I
now ſpeake of a conſtant louer indeed.

Inconſt. You may better ſpeake of him than finde him;
but the onely way to haue him,is,to be vnconſtant.

Conſt. How ſo ?

Inconſt. I haue heard Philoſophers ſay, that *Inquiſito ter-
mino ceſſat motus*, there is no motion (and you know
loue is a motion) but it ceaſeth (or rather dieth)
when it hath gotten his end; and to ſay the truth,
loue hath no edge when it is aſſured, whoſe verie

D   foode

foode and life is hope, and the hope of hauing, is
dull without the feare of looſing, where there are
no ryuals.

Conſt. But the more conſtant he findes me, the more
carefull he will be to deſerue well of me.

Inconſt. You deceiue your ſelfe with that conceite, and
giue him no ſmall aduantage to range where he li-
ſteth, when you let him know you are at his deuo-
tion, whom you ſhall be ſure to haue at yours, if by
an indifferent cariage of your ſelfe, you breede an
emulation betweene him and others.

Conſt. It were againſt nature for hir which is but one, to
loue more than one, and if it be a fault to beare a
double hart, what is it to diuide the hart among
many.

Inconſt. I aske no other iudge than nature, eſpecially in
this matter of loue, than which there is nothing
more naturall, and ſurely for any thing that I can
ſee, nature delighteth in nothing ſo much, as in va-
rietie; and it were hard, that ſince ſhe hath appoin-
ted varietie of colours for the eie, variety of ſounds
for the eare, varietie of meates for the mouth, and
varietie of other things for euery other ſenſe, ſhe
ſhould binde the hart (to which all the reſt doe ſer-
uice) to the loue of one any more, than ſhe bindeth
the eie to one colour, the eare to one ſound, or the
mouth to one kinde of meate.

Conſt. Neither doth ſhe deny the hart varietie of choyſe,
ſhe onely requires conſtancie when it hath choſen.

Inconſt. What if we commit an error in our choiſe?

Conſt. It is no fault to chooſe where we like.

Inconſt. But if our liking varie, may we not be better ad-
uiſed?

Conſt. When you haue once choſen, you muſt turne your
eies inward, to looke onelie on him whom you
haue placed in your hart.

Inconſt. Why then I perceiue you haue not yet choſen,

for

for your eies looke outwarde, but as long as your
eies ſtand in your head as they doe, I doubt not but
to finde you inconſtant.

Conſt. I do not denie but I looke vpon others beſide
him that I loue beſt, but they are all as dead pic-
tures vnto me, for any power they haue to touch
my hart.

Inconſt. If they were but (as you account them) dead pic-
tures, I do not doubt, but they would make an
other Pigmalion of you, rather than you would be
bound to the loue of one onely; but what if that
one prooue inconſtant?

Conſt. I had rather the fault ſhould be his than mine.

Inconſt. It is a ſmall comfort to ſay the fault is his, when
the loſſe is yours, but how can you auoid the fault,
who can helpe it and will not?

Conſt. I ſee no way to helpe it, but by breach of faith,
which I hold deerer then my life.

Inconſt. What is the band of your faith?

Conſt. My worde.

Inconſt. Your word is but winde, and no ſooner ſpoken
than gone.

Conſt. Yet doth it binde, to ſee what is ſpoken, done.

Inconſt. You can do little, if you cannot maſter your
worde.

Conſt. I ſhould do leſſe, if my word did not maſter me.

Inconſt. It maſters you indeed, for it makes you a ſlaue.

Conſt. To none but one, whom I chooſe to ſerue.

Inconſt. It is baſenes to ſerue, tho it be but one.

Conſt. More baſe to diſſemble with more than one.

Inconſt. When you loue all alike, you diſſemble with
none.

Conſt. But if I loue many, will any loue me?

Inconſt. No doubt there will, and ſo much the more, by
how much the more they are that ſtriue for you.

Conſt. But the hart that is euery where, is indeede no
where,

Inconſt. If you ſpeake of a mans hart, I grant it to be
true; but as for the hart of a woman, it is like a
ſoule in a bodie; *Tota in toto, & tota in qualibet parte* :
that though you had as many louers, as you haue
fingers and toes, you might be but one amongſt
them all, and yet wholy euery ones : but bicauſe I
ſee you are peruerſly deuoted to the cold ſinceri-
tie of imaginarie conſtancie, I leaue you to be as
you may, and purpoſe my ſelfe to be as I liſt : Ne-
uertheles, to your Maieſtie, by whom I haue ob-
tained this libertie, in token of my thankfulnes, I
offer this ſimple work of mine owne hands, which
you may weare as you pleaſe, but I made it after
mine owne minde to be worne looſe.

Conſt. And I who by your comming am not onely ſet at
libertie, but made partaker alſo of conſtancie, doe
preſent you with as vnworthie a worke of mine
owne hands, which yet I hope you will better ac-
cept, bicauſe it will ſerue to binde the looſnes of
that inconſtant dames token.

Inconſt. To binde the looſnes, and that of an inconſtant
dame, ſay no more than you know, for you knowe
not ſo much as I feele; well may we bewray our
ſelues betweene our ſelues, as thinking we haue
ſaid nothing, vntill we haue ſaide all. But now, a
greater power worketh in me, than your or my
reaſon, which draweth me from the circle of my
fancies, to the center of conſtant loue, there repre-
ſenting vnto me what contentment it is, to loue
but one, and how deſire is ſatiſfied with no num-
ber, when once it delighteth in more than one.

Conſt. I am not, I cannot be as I was, the leaue that I
did take of my ſelfe, is to leaue my ſelfe, and to
change, or rather to be changed to that eſtate
which admitteth no change : by the ſecret power
of hir, which though ſhe were content to let me be
caried almoſt out of breath with the winde of in-
conſtancie,

conſtancie, doth now in hir ſilence put me to ſi-
lence,and by the glorie of hir countenance, which
diſperſeth the flying cloudes of vaine conceites,
commands me too with others, and to be my ſelfe
as ſhe is, *Semper eadem.*

The Preamble to N.B.his Garden plot.

S Weete fellow whom I ſware, ſuch ſure affected loue,
As neither weale, nor woe, nor want,can from my minde re-
To thee my fellow ſweete,this wofull tale I tell,   (moue :
To let thee ſee the darke diſtreſſe, wherein my minde doth dwel.

On loathed bed I lay,my luſtleſſe lims to reſt,
Where ſtill I tumble to and fro,to ſeeke which ſide were beſt :
At laſt I catch a place, where long I cannot lie,
But ſtrange conceits from quiet ſleepes,do keep awake mine eie.

The time of yeere me ſeemes,doth bid me ſlouen riſe,
And not from ſhew of ſweete delight,to ſhut my ſleepie eies :
But ſorrow by and by, doth bid me ſlaue lie ſtill,
And ſlug amonſt the wretched ſouls,whom care doth ſeek to kil.

For ſorow is my ſpring, which brings forth bitter teares,
The fruits of friendſhip all forlorne,as feeble fancie feares.

A ſtrange deſcription of a rare Garden plot,
Written by N.B.Gent.

M Y garden ground of griefe:where ſelfe wils ſeeds are ſowne,
Whereof comes vp the weedes of wo, that ioies haue ouer-
With patience paled round to keep in ſecret ſpight :   (grown:
And quickſet round about with care,to keepe out all delight,
                               Foure

Foure quarters ſquared out,I finde in ſundrie ſort;
Whereof accordıng to their kindes,I meane to make report :
The firſt,the knot of loue,drawne euen by true deſier,
Like as it were two harts in one,and yet both would be nier.

The herbe is calde Iſop,the iuice of ſuch a taſte,
As with the ſowre,makes ſweete conceits to flie away too faſt :
The borders round about,are ſet with priuie ſweete,
Where neuer bird but nightingale,preſumde to ſet hir feete.

From this I ſtept aſide, vnto the knot of care,
Which ſo was croſt with ſtrange cōceits,as tong cannot declare:
The herbe was called Time,which ſet out all that knot :
And like a Maze me thought it was,when in the crookes I got.

The borders round about,are Sauerie vnſweete :
An herbe not much in my conceit,for ſuch a knot vnmeete :
From this to friendſhips knot,I ſtept and tooke the view,
How it was drawne,and then againe,in order how it grew.

The courſe was not vnlike,a kinde of hand in hand :
But many fingers were away,that there ſhould ſeeme to ſtand :
The herbe that ſet the knot,was Pennie Riall round :
And as me ſeem'd,it grew full cloſe,and nere vnto the ground.

And parched heere and there,ſo that it ſeemed not
Full as it ſhould haue been in deed, a perfeᴄt friendſhip knot :
Heerat I pawſd awhile,and tooke a little view
Of an od quarter drawne in beds,where herbs and flowers grew.

The flowres were buttons fine,for bȧtchelers to beare,
And by thoſe flowres ther grew an herb,was called maiden hear.

Amid this garden ground, a Condit ſtrange I found,
Which water fetcht from ſorows ſpring,to water al the ground:
To this my heauie houſe, the dungeon of diſtreſſe,
Where fainting hart lies panting ſtill,deſpairing of redreſſe.

                                                Whence

Whence from my window loe,this ſad proſpect I haue,
A piece of ground wheron to gaze,would bring one to his graue:
Lo thus the welcome ſpring,that others lends delight,
Doth make me die,to thinke I lie, thus drowned in deſpight,

That vp I cannot riſe,and come abrode to thee,
My fellow ſweet,with whom God knowes,how oft I wiſh to bee:
And thus in haſte adieu,my hart is growne ſo ſore,
And care ſo crookes my fingers ends,that I can write no more.

An excellent Dreame of Ladies and
their Riddles : by N.B.Gent.

IN Orchard grounds,where ſtore of fruit trees grew,
Me thought a Saint was walking all alone,
Of euerie tree,ſhe ſeemd to take hir view,
But in the end,ſhe plucked but of one :
　　This fruit quoth ſhe,doth like my fancie beſt :
　　Sweetings are fruit,but let that apple reſt.

Such fruit(quoth I)ſhall fancie chiefly feede :
Indeede tis faire,God grant it prooue as good,
But take good heede,leaſt all to late it breede
Ill humors ſuch as may infect your blood :
　　Yet take and taſte,but looke you know the tree :
　　Peace foole quoth ſhe,and ſo awaked mee.

What was this ground,wherein this dame did walke ?
And what was ſhe,that romed to and fro ?
And what ment I, to vſe ſuch kinde of talke ?
And what ment ſhe, to checke and ſnib me ſo ?
　　But what meane I ? alas,I was aſleepe :
　　Awake I ſweare,I will more ſilence keepe.

　　　　　　　　　　　　　　Well

Well thus I wakte and fell asleepe againe :
And then I fell into another vaine.

Great wars me thought grew late by strange mishap,
Desire had stolne out of Dianaes traine,
Hir darling deere, and laid on Venus lap,
Who, Cupid sware should neuer backe againe.
   Ere he would so loose all his harts delight,
   He vow'd to die, wherewith began a fight.

Diana shot, and Cupid shot againe :
Fame sounded out hir trumpe with heauenly cheare :
Hope was ill hurt, despite was onely slaine :
Diana forst in fine for to retire.
   Cupid caught fame, and brought hir to his frend :
   The trumpet ceast, and so my dreame did end.

Thus scarce awake, I fell asleepe againe,
And then I was within a garden ground,
Beset with flowres, the allies euen and plaine :
And all the banks beset with roses round,
   And sundrie flowres so super sweete of smell,
   As there me thought it was a heauen to dwell.

Where walking long, anon I gan espie
Sweete pretie soules, that pluckt ech one a flowre :
When from their sight I hid me by and by,
Behinde a banke within a brier bowre :
   Where after walke, I saw them where they sat :
   Beheld their hues, and heard their pretie chat :

Sister quoth one, how shall we spend this day ?
Deuise (quoth she) some pretie merie iest :
Content quoth one, beshrew them that say nay :
Some purposes or riddles I thinke best :
   Riddles cried all, and so the sport begun :
   Forfet a fillop, she that first hath done.

Loe thus a while was curtſey to propound,
Yet in the end this order did they take,
By two and two, they ſhould ſit cloſe and round;
And one begin, another anſwere make :
    Whoſe ridling ſports in order as I can,
    I will recite, and thus the firſt began.

The firſt Riddle.

Within a gallant plot of ground,
There growes a flowre that hath no name,
The like whereof was neuer found,
And none but one can plucke the ſame :
    Now where this ground or flowre doth growe,
    Or who that one, tis hard to knowe.

The Anſwere.

Siſter (quoth ſhe) if thou wouldſt knowe
This ground, this flowre, and happie man,
Walke in this garden to and fro :
Here you ſhall ſee them now and than :
    Which when you finde to your delight,
    Then thinke I hit your riddle right.

The ſecond Riddle.

Within a field there growes a flowre,
That decks the ground where as it growes,
It ſprings and falls, both in an howre,
And but at certaine times it ſhowes :
    It neuer dies, and ſeldome ſeene,
    And tis a Noſegay for a Queene.

The Anſwere.

This field is fauor, Grace the ground,
Whence ſprings the flowre of curteſie,

E   Soone

Soone growne and gone though ſomtime found,
Not dead, but hid, from flattrers eie,
    That pickthanks may not plucke the ſame :
    Thus haue I red your riddle Dame.

The third Riddle.

Within a flowre a ſeede there growes,
Which ſomtime falls, but ſeldome ſprings,
And if it ſpring, it ſeldome blowes,
And if it blowe, no ſweete it brings,
    And therefore counted but a weede :
    Now geſſe the flowre, and what the ſeede.

The Anſwere.

In fancies flowre is ſorrowes ſeede,
Which ſomtimes falls, but ſprings but ſeeld,
And if it ſpring, tis but a weede,
Which doth no ſweete, nor ſauor yeeld,
    And yet the flowre, both faire and ſweete,
    And for a Princes garden meete.

The fourth Riddle.

Within a ſeede doth poiſon lurke,
Which onely Spiders feede vpon,
And yet the Bee can wiſely woorke,
To ſucke out honie, poiſon gone :
    Which honie, poiſon, Spider, Bee,
    Are hard to geſſe, yet eath to ſee.

The Anſwere.

In ſorrowes ſeede is ſecret paine,
Which ſpite the Spider onely ſucks,
Which poiſon gone, then wittie braine
The wilie Bee, hir honie plucks,

And

And beares it to hir hiue vnhurt,
When spider trod, dies in the durt.

Gramercie wench (quoth she) that first begoon,
Each one me seemes hath quit hir selfe right well,
And now since that our riddles all are doon,
Let vs go sing the flowre of sweetest smell :
   Well may it fare, wherewith each tooke a part,
   And thus they soong, all with a merie hart.

Blest be the ground that first brought forth the flowre,
Whose name vntolde, but vertues not vnknowne :
Happie the hand, whom God shall giue the powre,
To plucke this flowre, and take it for his owne :
   Oh heauenly stalke, that staines all where it growes :
   From whom more sweet, than sweetest hony flowes.

Oh sweete of sweetes, the sweetest sweete that is :
Oh flowre of flowres, that yeelds so sweete a sent :
Oh sent so sweete, as when the head shall misse :
Oh heauens what hart but that will sore lament :
   God let thee spring, and flourish so each howre,
   As that our sweetes may neuer turne to sowre.

For we with sweetes doe feede our fancies so,
With sweetes of sight, and sweetnes of conceit,
That we may wish that it may euer groe,
Amid delights where we desire to wait,
   Vpon the flowre that pleaseth euerie eie,
   And glads each hart ; God let it neuer die.

Wherewith me thought alowd I cride, Amen :
And therewithall I started out of sleepe :
Now what became of these faire Ladies then,
I cannot tell, in minde I onely keepe
   These ridling toies which heere I doe recite :
   Ile tell ye more perhaps another night.

       The

The Chesse Play.

Very aptly deuised by N. B. Gent.

A Secret many yeeres vnseene,
   In play at Chesse, who knowes the game,
   First of the King, and then the Queene,
Knight, Bishop, Rooke, and so by name,
   Of euerie Pawne I will descrie,
   The nature with the qualitie.

The King.

The King himselfe is haughtie Care,
Which ouerlooketh all his men,
And when he seeth how they fare,
He steps among them now and then,
   Whom, when his foe presumes to checke,
   His seruants stand, to giue the necke.

The Queene.

The Queene is queint, and quicke Conceit,
Which makes hir walke which way she list,
And rootes them vp, that lie in wait
To worke hir treason, ere she wist :
   Hir force is such against hir foes,
   That whom she meetes, she ouerthrowes.

The Knight.

The Knight is knowledge how to fight
Against his Princes enimies,
He neuer makes his walke outright,
But leaps and skips, in wilie wise,
   To take by sleight a traitrous foe,
   Might slilie seeke their ouerthrowe.

The

The Bishop.

The Bishop he is wittie braine,
That chooseth Crossest pathes to pace,
And euermore he pries with paine,
To see who seekes him most disgrace :
    Such straglers when he findes astraie,
    He takes them vp, and throwes awaie.

The Rookes.

The Rookes are reason on both sides,
Which keepe the corner houses still,
And warily stand to watch their tides,
By secret art to worke their will,
    To take sometime a theefe vnseene,
    Might mischiefe meane to King or Queene.

The Pawnes.

The Pawne before the king, is peace,
Which he desires to keepe at home,
Practise, the Queenes, which doth not cease
Amid the world abroad to roame,
    To finde, and fall vpon each foe,
    Whereas his mistres meanes to goe.

Before the knight, is perill plast,
Which he, by skipping ouergoes,
And yet that Pawne can worke a cast,
To ouerthrow his greatest foes ;
    The Bishops, prudence, prieng still,
    Which way to worke his masters will.

The Rookes poore Pawnes, are sillie swaines,
Which seeldome serue, except by hap,

                      And

And yet thoſe Pawnes, can lay their traines,
To catch a great man, in a trap :
    So that I ſee, ſometime a groome
    May not be ſpared from his roome.

The nature of the Cheſſe men.

The King is ſtately, looking hie ;
The Queene, doth beare like maieſtie :
The Knight, is hardie, valiant, wiſe :
The Biſhop, prudent, and preciſe :
    The Rookes, no raungers out of raie,
    The Pawnes, the pages in the plaie.

L E N V O Y.

Then rule with care, and quicke conceit,
And fight with knowledge, as with force ;
So beare a braine, to daſh deceit,
And worke with reaſon and remorſe :
    Forgiue a fault, when yoong men plaie,
    So giue a mate, and go your way.

And when you plaie beware of Checke,
Know how to ſaue and giue a necke :
And with a Checke, beware of Mate ;
But cheeſe, ware had I wiſt too late :
    Looſe not the *Queene*, for ten to one,
    If ſhe be loſt, the game is gone.

A

A moſt rare, and excellent Dreame, lear-
nedly ſet downe by a woorthy Gentleman,
*a braue Scholler, and M. of Artes
in both Vniuerſities.*

THe while we ſleepe, whereof may it proceed,
    Our minde is led with dreames of diuers ſorts,
    Some fearfull things, and diſcontentment breede,
Some merriment, and pretie idle ſports,
And ſome of future things preſage imports;
    Some wounds the conſcience with the former gilt,
    Of outrage, wrongs, and bloud vniuſtly ſpilt.

Some ſtrange effects if not impoſſible,
As to be caried in the emptie aire,
Of transformations ſome incredible,
From forme to forme, and of their backe repaire,
Some pleaſant ſhewes preſents, and ſome diſpaire:
    Some grauer things a ſleeping can diſcuſſe:
    And other, matters meere ridiculous.

Men diuerſly do argue of the cauſe
Of dreames: Some their occaſion thus recites,
The while the bodie takes his needfull pauſe,
In ſleepe to freſh and to reſtore the ſprites,
Decaid by labor, or the daies delites,
    The minde, the cogitations of the day do keepe,
    And run them ouer when we are aſleepe.

Others our meates do charge with thoſe effects
That indigeſted in the ſtomacke lies:
Other celeſtiall influence reſpects,
And fetch from them our ſleeping fantaſies;
The which they recommend as Propheſies:
    For when our ſprites are ſtirred with thoſe charms,
    We are foretold of good or future harms.
                                        But

But this coniecture cheefly I embrace,
Euen as the ſea enraged with the winde,
After the ſtorme alaid will mooue a ſpace,
The ſelfe ſame reaſon may be well aſſignde,
Vnto the nightly labors of the minde :
　　Who works in ſleepe,our actions at a ſtay,
　　Vpon th'occaſions of the paſſed day.

Vpon a dreame I had, I this prefer,
The which the ſequell ſhall deliuer ſtraite :
That Loue that firſt did make my reaſon erre,
Straitly one day commanded me to waite,
On paine to pine,and periſh in conceite ;
　　Vpon my ſoueraigne, vnto whom I went,
　　As dutie wild,and Loues commandement.

Mine eies,the firſt intreating meſſengers,
By ſignes of ſorrow openly did ſpeake,
After my toong the humble ſuite prefers
Of my poore hart,with torments like to breake :
But little of my ſuffrings doth ſhe reake :
　　Sooner the rocks their hardnes will forgo,
　　Than ſhe acknowledge that which ſhe doth know.

In fine,vnto my chamber I retire,
A thouſand fancies hamring on my wits,
Deſpaire,griefe,anguiſh,furie,and deſire,
Doe exerciſe in turne their Bedlem fits,
Whereof to ſpeake,or heare,beſt them befits,
　　That now enioyeng,heretofore haue tride,
　　The hell,and bitternes of Loue denide.

By this the night doth through the skie diſplay
Hir ſable robe,ſpangled with golden ſtars,
And voiceleſſe ſilence gan to chace away
Noyſes and ſounds,with their moleſting iars :
And ſo the place to needfull ſleepe prepars ;

　　　　　　　　　　　　　　　　Who

Who Motherlike,moſt tenderly aſſwages,
The daies aggreeuances and damages.

Encumbred thus,I went vnto my bed,
Loue knowes,with litle hope of taking reſt,
Fancie and frenzie worketh on my head,
One while the one,then th'other gets the beſt:
Now eithers faction egarly addreſt;
　　To hoſtile conflict furiouſly diſcend,
　　Of purpoſe ſtrait to make a finall end.

Extremitie proceeding on ſo far,
When eithers forces equally were ſpent,
They ſtinted of themſelues this raging war,
And left with victorie indifferent :
Slumber that found the time conuenient,
　　Seeing the ſlacknes of their wearied traine,
　　Vpon th'aduantage ſeaſed on my braine.

Who holding me vnder his ſhadie wings,
To mitigate the anguiſh of my thought,
Preſented me with diuers pleaſant things,
Amongſt the reſt,a Ladie faire he brought,
Frō heauen no doubt thoſe features there are wrought,
　　Whoſe raies of beautie admirable bright,
　　Filled my chamber with a Sunſhine light.

Hir Amber treſſes on hir ſhoulders lies,
The which as ſhe doth moue,diuided run,
About hir bodie iuſt in circle wiſe,
Like to the curious web Arachne ſpun;
Or elſe to make a fit compariſon,
　　Like ſlender twiſt turned to ſhining fire,
　　Or flames by woonder wrought into a wire.

The forehead that confines theſe burniſht haires,
For whitenes ſtriueth with vntouched ſnowe;
　　　　　　F　　　　　　　　　For

For ſmoothnes with the Iuorie compares;
And doth the Alablaſters gliſtring ſhowe,
Vnder this firmament you are to know,
 Two powrfull ſtars which at their pleaſure moue,
 The variable effects that followes loue.

Hir cheekes reſembleth right a garden plot,
Of diuers ſorts of rare Carnation flowres,
The which the ſcortching Sun offendeth not,
Nor boyſtrous winter with his rotting ſhowres;
Vncertaine Iuno thereon neuer lowres:
 Heere Venus with hir little loues repoſes,
 Amongſt the lillies and the damaske roſes.

Hir lips compares with the Vermilion morne,
Hir equall teeth in ſemicircle wiſe,
For orientnes ſelected pearle may ſcorne,
What may I of hir iſſuing breath deuiſe,
That from this pearle and Synaber doth riſe:
 The francumſence and myrr,that Inde preſents,
 Within this aire leeſe their extolled ſents.

The noſe,the chin,the ſtraight erected necke,
Supporter to the head : next ſhoulders ſtands,
The which diſcends into the arme direct,
And terminates their length vpon the hands :
At each of theſe my wits amaſed ſtands :
 For when I would their merits vtter foorth,
 I finde all words inferior to their woorth.

The garments wherewithall ſhe was attyrde,
But ſlender in account,and yet were more
Than hir perfections needfully requyrde,
Whoſe euery part hath of contentment ſtore :
But as it was,thanks to my dreame therefore,
 Who cauſde the apparition to be wrought,
 As all lay open to mine eies or thought.

         There

There was, as I obſeru'd next to hir skin,
A ſnowe white lawne, tranſparent as the aire,
And ouer this a garment wondrous thin,
Of networke, wrought in blacke, exceeding faire;
Whoſe masks were ſmall, and thred as fine as haire,
 Girt with a tawnie Cyprous were hir clothes,
 And thus attirde, this Angell woman goes.

Hir mouing breſts as equall Promontories,
Diuided by an Indraft from the maine,
Doe imitate the gently moued Seas,
That riſing fall, and falling riſe againe:
As they, ſo did my life in euery vaine:
 My ſpirit iſſued as they waxed hier,
 And as they ſetled, backe againe retier.

Next neighbor heerunto in due diſcent,
Hir bellie plaine, the bed of nameleſſe bliſſe,
Wherein all things appeere aboue content,
And paradiſe is nothing more than this:
In which Deſire was mou'd to doe amiſſe;
 For when his eies vpon this tree was caſt,
 O blame him not, if he requirde to taſte.

What followed this, I cannot well report:
The tawnie Cyprous that forehanging fell,
Reſtraind mine eies in moſt malitious ſort,
Which of themſelues were elſe affected well,
Although as witnes nought thereof I tell:
 I doubt not thoſe that fine conceited be,
 Sees ſomwhat further, than mine eies might ſee.

But of hir praiſes thus in generall,
Deſirde perfection ſhewd in euerie part,
Yet all appeerd in each one ſeuerall,
Vnto the wonder of the eie and hart,
Of euery priuate part to write apart.
   F 2   Were

Were worke and argument for him that vſes,
The daily conuerſation of the Muſes.

Who this ſhould be,if any long to heare,
I ſay it is the portraict of the Saint,
Which deepe ingraued in my hart I beare,
The Miſtres of my hope,my feare, and plaint,
And thou that with hir praiſes I acquaint,
    If thou canſt nothing elſe,yet wiſh thou me,
    Deliuerd of that beauties crueltie.

With vnperceiued motion drawing ny,
Vnto the bed of my diſtreſſe and feare,
She with hir hand doth put the curtaine by,
And ſits hir downe vpon the one ſide there :
My waſted ſpirits quite amazed were,
    To ſee the ſudden morning of thoſe eies,
    Within the darke thus inexpected riſe.

Being abrode (quoth ſhe) I lately hard,
That you were falne into a ſudden feuer,
And ſolitarie in your chamber bard,
From companie you did your ſelfe diſſeuer,
To charitie it appertaineth euer,
    In duties to our neighbors for to ſticke,
    And viſit the afflicted and the ſicke.

Which Chriſtian office hither hath me led,
Wiſhing I could recouerie to you bring,
Ladie (quoth I) as eaſly done as ſed,
For you that haue my life in managing,
What need you wiſh,when you may doe the thing :
    For if you be diſpoſd to charitie,
    Beſtowe on me this wiſht recouerie.

Is't in my garden that may doe thee good ?
(Quoth ſhe)or in my cloſet of conſerues,

                      Or

Or may my kitchin any kinde of foode
Deuiſe, that to thy taſte and fancie ſerues,
Ladie (ſaid I) no coolice, no conſerues,
    No herbe, no potion commeth nie that part,
    That ſuffereth this anguiſh and this ſmart.

When further I would faine haue ſpoken on,
With fearfulnes I felt my toong reſtrained,
And ſhamefaſtnes with red Vermilion,
My ſhallow cheekes and countenance diſtained :
Now by this meanes my hart more deepely pained,
    Sent out a flood of weeping to betoken,
    The reſt of that my toong had left vnſpoken.

As ſoone as ſighes had ouerblowne my teares,
And teares allaid my ſighings vehemence,
Audacitie expulſer of thoſe feares,
Gaue to deſire at laſt preheminence,
Who ſaw it now to be of conſequence;
    Sauced his tale with dutie and reſpeɛ̃t,
    And thus began, or to the like effeɛ̃t.

It is no feuer (Ladie) in the vaines,
Nor in the blood, of humors the exceſſe,
Nor ſtomacks vapor, that annoies the braines,
Nor ill contagion in the Arteries,
Nor any griefe that Phyſicke remedies :
    It is, &c. and heere my lips refuſde to moue,
    Stopping the ſentence ere I came to Loue.

Haply (ſaid ſhe) as I doe iudge thereon,
It is ſome toy or fancie in your head,
Some ſicknes grounded on opinion,
Or elſe ſome error your conceit hath bred :
Then as ſuppoſe you to this anguiſh led,
    By mine aduice, if you liſt ruled be,
    For health ſake doe ſuppoſe the contrarie.
                                        Were

Were it within the compas of my wits,
(Leader of my defires)thus I replide,
To remedie the outrage of thofe fits,
That from this bodie would my life diuide,
The rather fhould thefe cordials be applide,
    That I might keepe my life in health,to doe,
    The feruices that loue commands me to.

But out alas,that waied downe with paine,
With hands erected vp,that I fhould crie,
As doth the faylers blowne into the maine,
After the fhip that fore the winde doth flie,
And yet in fight of helpe,muft helpeles die:
    So I,neere hir that can my woes appeafe,
    Doe perifh like the outcaft in the Seas.

Are you the woorfer that I am fo neere,
The Ladie faid, and I not thereof ware?
Nay happie then(quoth I) that you are heere,
And haples too,bicaufe you are fo farre:
She aunfwered hereunto, thefe riddles are:
    Can neere be far,can happy haples be?
    As well(quoth I)as fee,and not to fee.

What is he(Madame)that doth baite his eies,
Be he of mortall or immortall kinde,
Vpon the beauties which your vifage dies,
And drawes not prefent death into his minde,
Vnles your gratious lookes do prooue fo kinde,
    As with a yeelding fauour to preuent,
    The dangers thereunto are incident.

Can it be poffible you fhould not knowe
The powre and vertue of fweete beauties gift?
Can heauen and nature meafureles beftowe
The things that you to Angels calling lift?
And you not vnderftand their purpof'd drift?

                           Might

Might they aduance yee to a Goddeſſe ſeate,
And you be ignorant why they make yee great?

If this were true, which you of me ſuppoſe,
The praiſe of beautie, and commended parts,
I ſee no reaſon to eſteeme of thoſe,
That do complaine them of ſuch pettie ſmarts,
Not incident to men of valiant harts :
　　The argument is dull, and nothing quicke,
　　Bicauſe that I am faire, you ſhould be ſicke.

Suppoſe I haue thoſe graces and thoſe flowres,
And all the vertues that you can recite,
You looke, you like, and you muſt haue them yours;
Forſooth, bicauſe they mooue your appetite :
I ſee no reaſon to impart my right,
　　Before that God and men agreed be,
　　To let all things run in communitie.

An eaſie thing for you to ouercome,
(Faire Ladie)him, that is ſo deepe your thrall :
For euery ſyllable from your lips that come,
Beares wit, and weight, and vehemence withall :
Vnder the which, my ſubiect ſpirits fall :
　　If you do ſpeake, or if you nought expreſſe,
　　Your beautie of it ſelfe is Conquereſſe.

With fauour (Ladie) giue me leaue to ſpeake,
(If you will liſten a condemneds tale)
No pettie wound can make my hart ſtrings breake :
Nor might a trifle worke this deadly bale :
Your ſoueraigne beautie doth me hither hale :
　　The ſtronger doth (euen by a common courſe)
　　Ouer the weaker exerciſe his force.

Ladie, in condiſcending vnto Loue,
You do not ſhare nor yet your right forgo,

In

In that you ſhall your ſeruants ſute approue,
And bleſſe him with thoſe fauors you can ſhowe,
To higher place of dignitie you growe :
    The Sun were not in my opinion bright,
    If there were not eie witnes of his light.

No abieƈt commons of thoſe things he ſeekes,
Nor any way doth labor to induce
That liues to ſerue and honor hir he leekes,
In hope at laſt to make an happie truce,
And for this cauſe all other he refuſe :
    To exerciſe thoſe parts with ſerious care,
    Which to his Miſtres fancie pleaſing are.

But ſir (quoth ſhe)how can ye anſwere this ?
You men complaine,Loues torments to be great;
Saying that he a mightie Tyrant is;
Such one as putteth reaſon from hir ſeat;
Why wiſh ye to inſnare me in this net ?
    Better it is you ſuffer that you doe,
    Then ſuch extreames ſhould happen vpon two.

When Loue (ſweete Ladie)thorowly accords,
The Louers and beloueds harts in one,
This amitie a perfeƈt heauen affords,
Vpon the inſtant of this vnion :
Baniſht is thence all ſorrow,care,and mone,
    For they which in conſpiring Loue abide,
    Liue with continuall ioies, vnſatisfide.

This is beleeu'd and knowne by common brute,
When of vs Dames ye hap to get a graunt,
You giue it to the cunning of your ſute,
Vſing with your companions thus to vaunt :
Theſe pretie fooles,tis nothing to enchaunt :
    As fiſhers vſe for fiſh, with fiſh to bait,
    Theſe faire ones,ſo,faire ſpeeches catches ſtrait.

                                   Let

Let not(ſweete Loue)the fault of one or few,
Or ſiniſter report of trutheleſſe famé,
Endamage the deſart of him can ſhew
Many effects repugnant to the ſame,
Vnworthie he of life, or Louers name,
    Shall dare vnto hir honor,wrong,or ſcathe,
    Of whom both life,and happines he hathe.

It is a proofe(ſaid ſhe)of fooliſhnes,
To ſet that vpon chaunce which may be ſure,
Exempt from Loue,I liue in happines,
In which condition I will yet indure :
Griefes come apace,we neede not them procure :
    In the eſtate I liue,I am content,
    And minde not Loue,in dread of diſcontent.

I know(quoth I)you can from Loue refraine,
Bicauſe he holds his ſtate within your eies :
But I,the vaſſall of his hard diſdaine,
Am ſo deiected,as I cannot riſe ;
Albeit my ſute and ſeruice you diſpiſe,
    Yet giue me leaue to honor and admire,
    Your beautie which afflicteth my deſire.

Ther's little reaſon (ſaid ſhe then)to like
The thing which you affirme to vexe ye ſo,
If your deſire ſuch diſcontentment ſtrike,
Such war,ſuch anguiſh,agonies,and woe,
Let that fantaſtike I aduiſe ye goe :
    The man is much deſirous of vnreſt,
    That home intreates a knowne diſquiet gueſt.

Excepting Loue,demaund you at my hand,
What euer is in my abilitie :
And may with vertue,and mine honor ſtand,
Ladie(ſaid I)Loue is the Maladie,
And vnto Loue,Loue's th'onely remedie :
                    G   But

But ſith you doe herein my ſute deteſt,
Then grant me this, the laſt I ſhall requeſt.

When haples Loue hath brought me to the graue,
If ſo at any time you paſſe that way,
Where my conſuming bones their buriall haue,
Vouchſafe yee then for pitties ſake to ſay,
As I remember, heere my ſeruant lay,
    Long time a Louer in affection true,
    Whom my diſdaine and rigor ouerthrew.

Altho yee die (quoth ſhe) I will not loue,
And for you will not loue (ſaid I) I die:
Then preſently my ſpirits faild to moue,
Retiring backe themſelues ſucceſſiuelie:
But when ſhe did the ſigne of death eſpie,
    She puld, ſhe halde, ſeruant (ſaid ſhe) abide,
    Let not thy miſtres be thy homicide.

If thy affections doe from Loue proceede,
How canſt thou die, and I thy liues life neere?
If thou dooſt loue, and honor me indeede,
Why with this act doſt thou defame me heere?
If thou eſteemſt my Loue and honor deere,
    O liue, and ſee my rigour ouerthrowne,
    And come and take poſſeſſion of thine owne.

And then vnable weeping to withholde,
She ſundrie meanes aſſaies to make me liue,
My breſts ſhe ſtrikes, ſhe rubs my temples colde,
And with ſuch vehemence of labours ſtriue,
As life vnto a Marble ſtone might giue:
    My hand at laſt, ſhe amorouſly doth ſtraine,
    And with a kiſſe drew vp my life againe.

This new ſprong ioy conceiued in my hart,
Of Loues aſſurance vnder hand and ſeale,

                     Dilated

Dilated thence abroad to euery part,
Telling how graciouſlie my loue did deale,
My ſoule and ſpirit ſwelling with this zeale,
    So rowſed ſleepe, that he his holde forſooke,
    And I through ſurfeit of the ioy awooke.

Awaked thus, I preſently perceiu'd,
The vanitie and falſhood of theſe ioyes;
Finding that fond illuſions had deceiu'd
My ouerwatched braine with idle toyes;
Then I that freſhly felt my firſt annoyes,
    Their woonted rage within my thoughts to keepe,
    Gan thus expoſtulate the cauſe with ſleepe.

Thou eaſe of harts, with burth'nous woes oppreſt,
Thou pitier of the cares of buſie daie,
Thou friend to louers in their deepe vnreſt,
Turning their anguiſhes another waie,
Why may not I continue with thee aie,
    Sith that my deſtinie is ſo extreame,
    As not to haue my good, but in a dreame.

Why art thou not (O dreame) the ſame you ſeeme?
Seeing thy viſions our contentment brings;
Or doe we of their woorthines miſdeeme?
To call them ſhadowes that are reall things?
And falſlie attribute their due to wakings?
    O doe but then perpetuate thy ſleight,
    And I will ſweare, thou workſt not by deceit.

And now the Morning entring at the glaſſe,
Made of theſe thoughts ſome intermiſſion:
Thus haue I tolde what things in dreame did paſſe,
Vpon the former daies occaſion;
And whence they come in mine opinion;
    But whether they tell truth, or nothing leſſe,
    I ſhall reſolue, vpon my dreames ſucceſſe.

Excellent

Excellent Ditties of diuers kindes, and
rare inuention : written by
sundry Gentlemen.

WEepe you my lines for sorrow whilst I write,
For you alone may manifest my griefe,
Your numbers must my endles woes recite,
Such woes as wound my soule without reliefe,
  Such bitter woes, as who so would disclose them,
  Must cease to talke, for hart can scarse suppose them.

My restles braines deuour'd by many thoughts,
Disclaiming ioies doth make a heauen of hell,
An Idoll of mislikes, a God of noughts,
Contrarious passions on my braine doth dwell,
  They would haue ease, yet seeke for ceaslesse strife,
  And make their cause of death, their meanes of life.

Mine eies are dim'd by two diuine delights,
And through their sight, my hart hath caught a wound:
Their lids were shut amids the lingring nights :
Their yeelding fountaines watring of the ground,
  Doe ceasles run, and shroud their shining ioy,
  And drowne Content in riuers of annoy.

I faine to smile, when as I faint for feare :
I dreame on ioy, when as I doubt of woe :
I burne in fire, yet still approch it neare :
I like of mirth, yet will no solace knowe :
  I see content, yet neuer cease to sigh :
  I liue secure, yet danger passeth nigh.

I catch at hope,yet ouertake it neuer :
I feede on thought,yet thought doth force my end :
I craue repofe,yet finde difquiet euer :
I fcorne aduice,yet counfell is my frend :
    I will be free,yet feede on thraldome ſtill :
    I honor wit,yet feede on foolifh will.

Mine eies complaine the follies of my hart :
My hart laments the errors of mine eie :
My thoughts would burie endles things in art :
Mine eie,my hart,my thoughts,wend all awrie :
    Yet of my harmes(ye heauens)the worſt is this ;
    I cannot cenfure what my forrow is.

My life is death,for no delights are in it :
My mufike mone,and yet I neuer leaue it :
My fuccour hope,yet can I neuer win it :
My gaines report,yet will I not perceiue it :
    My foode fufpect,and yet I cannot flie it :
    My foe neglect,and yet I meane to trie it.

By day I freeze,I frie, I wifh,I wait :
By night I loath my reſt, and wifh for day :
Both day and night,my hart with doubts I bait :
Weying delight from caufe of my decaie :
    The Vultures that confume my tender breſt,
    Is fweete defire,the caufe of my vnreſt.

Now what I am,my forie cheekes difclofe :
Once what I was, my fmiling eies bewraid :
Now what I want,conjecture by my woes :
Once what I fcornd, hath now my hart betraid :
    Wo's me,my want of helpe doth well approue,
    The paines I feele,is euen the pangs of Loue.

Well,be it paine, Loues torments let it be :
Let endles thoughts confume my reſtles braines :

                    Let

Let teares ſo choake mine eies, I may not ſee :
Let toong be mute, for to diſcloſe my paines :
   Let ioyes, let hope, let all contents ſurceaſe,
   Theſe bitter plagues, my fancies ſhall increaſe.

No paine, no fortune ſhall my Loue confound :
My ſpotles faith, my ſimple truth ſhall proue,
That I my liking on no errors ground :
Thus will I liue, thus will I paſſe my Loue :
   Repulſe, contempt, can neuer alter kinde;
   Loues triumph doth conſiſt in conſtant minde.

With conſtant minde the poore remainder gift,
That Loue amongſt his many ſpoyles hath left me,
Is that which to the heauens my face ſhall lift,
Though other hope by fortune be bereft me;
   And if I die, this praiſe ſhall me awair,
   My Loue was endleſſe, voide of all deceit.

F I N I S.

MVſes helpe me, ſorrow ſwarmeth,
Eies are fraught with ſeas of languiſh,
Haples hope my ſolace harmeth :
Mindes repaſt is bitter anguiſh.

Eie of daie regarded neuer,
Certaine truſt in world vntruſtie,
Flattring hope beguileth euer :
Wearie olde, and wanton luſtie.

Dawne of day, beholdes inthroned,
Fortunes darling proud and dreadles :
Darkſome night doth heare him moned,
Who before was rich and needles.

Rob the ſpheare of lines vnited;
Make a ſudden voide in nature :

Force

Force the day to be benighted;
Reaue the cause of time, and creature.

Ere the world will cease to varie :
This I weepe for, this I sorrow :
Muses if you please to tarie,
Further helpe I meane to borrow.

Courted once by fortunes fauor,
Compast now with enuies curses :
All my thoughts of sorrowes sauor,
Hopes run fleeting like the Sourses.

Ay me wanton scorne hath maimed
All the ioies my hart enioied :
Thoughts their thinking haue disclaimed,
Hate my hopes haue quite annoied.

Scant regard my weale hath scanted :
Looking coie hath forst my lowring :
Nothing likte, where nothing wanted,
Weds mine eies to ceasles showring.

Former Loue was once admired,
Present fauor is estranged :
Loath'd the pleasure long desired;
Thus both men and thoughts are changed.

Louely Swaine with luckie speeding,
Once (but now no more) so frended :
Thou my flocks hast had in feeding,
From the morne, till day was ended.

Drinke and fodder, foode and folding,
Had my lambes and ewes togeather :
I with them was still beholding,
Both in warmth, and winter weather.

                                    Now

Now they languiſh ſince refuſed,
Ewes and lambes are paind with pining :
I with ewes and lambes confuſed,
All vnto our deathes declining.

Silence leaue thy caue obſcured,
Daine a dolefull Swaine to tender,
Though diſdaines I haue endured,
Yet I am no deepe offender.

Philips ſonne can with his finger,
Hide his ſcar, it is ſo little :
Little ſinne a day to linger,
Wiſe men wander in a tittle.

Trifles yet my Swaine haue turned,
Tho my ſonne he neuer ſhoweth :
Tho I weepe, I am not mourned,
Tho I want, no pitie groweth.

Yet for pitie loue my muſes,
Gentle ſilence be their couer,
They muſt leaue their wonted vſes,
Since I leaue to be a Louer.

They ſhall liue with thee incloſed,
I will loath my pen and paper :
Art ſhall neuer be ſuppoſed,
Sloth ſhall quench the watching taper.

Kiſſe them ſilence, kiſſe them kindely,
Tho I leaue them, yet I loue them :
Tho my wit haue led them blindely,
Yet my Swaine did once approue them.

I will trauell ſoiles remoued,
Night and morning neuer merie,

                              Thou

Thou ſhalt harbor that I loued,
I will loue that makes me wearie.

If perchaunce the Shepherd ſtraieth,
In thy walks and ſhades vnhaunted,
Tell the Teene my hart betraieth,
How negle&t my ioyes haue daunted.

T. L. Gent.

STriue no more,
Forſpoken ioyes to ſpring :
Since care hath clipt thy wing :
    But ſtoope thoſe lampes before :
That nurſt thee vp at firſt,with friendly ſmiles,
And now through ſcornes thy truſt beguiles.

    Pine away ,
That pining you may pleaſe;
For death betides you eaſe :
    Oh ſweete and kinde decay;
To pine and die,whilſt Loue giues looking on,
And pines to ſee your pining mone.

    Dying ioyes,
Your ſhrine is conſtant hart,
That glories in his ſmart :
    Your Tropheis are annoyes,
And on your tombe,by Loue theſe lines are plaſte,
Loe heere they lie,whom ſcorne defaſte.

T. L. Gent.

OF ceaſles thoughts my mind hath fram'd his wings,
Wherewith he ſoares and climes aboue conceit,
And midſt his flight for endles ioy he ſings,
To ſpie thoſe double lampes,whoſe ſweete receit
        H   Muſt

Muſt be the heauen where as my ſoule ſhall reſt,
Though by their ſhine my bodie be depreſt.

Hir eies ſhrowd pitie, pietie, and pure,
Hir face ſhields Roſes, Lillies, and delight,
Hir hand hath powre, to conquere and allure,
Hir hart, holds honor, loue, remorce, and right,
 Hir minde is fraught, with wiſdome, faith, and loue,
 All what is hirs, is borrowed from aboue.

Then mount my minde, and feare no future fall,
Exceed conceit, for ſhe exceeds conceit ꝛ
Burne louely lamps, to whom my lookes are thrall,
My ſoule ſhall glorie in ſo ſweete receit,
 Tho in your flames my corſe to cinders wend,
 Yet am I proud to gaine a Phœnix end.

T. L. Gent.

WHen Pirrha made hir miracle of ſtones,
 The baſer ſort of flintie molde ſhe fram'd,
Whoſe courſe compaƈt concealed all at once,
All what in nature could imperfeƈt be,
 So but imperfeƈt perfeƈt, was the ſhape,
And minde euen with the mettall did agree.

 The finer formes of Diamonds ſhe made,
 A peereles ſubſtance matchles for the molde,
 Whence grew ſuch ſhapes that heauen his pure for-
To frame a minde agreeing to the forme.   (ſook,

This by my proofe, I finde for certaine true,
For why my miſtres matchles in hir ſhape,
For bodie farre exceeds my baſe report,
 For minde, no minde can craue more rare ſupplies,
 And laſt I ſpie the Saphirs in hir eies,

T. L. Gent.

All

ALl day I weepe my wearie woes,
Then when that night approcheth neere,
And euery one his eies doth cloſe,
And paſſed paines no more appeere,
　　　　　　　I change my cheere,

And in the weepings of mine eie,
Loue bathes his wings,and from my hart
Drawes fire his furie to ſupplie,
And on my bones doth whet his dart:
　　　　　　　Oh bitter ſmart.

My ſighes within their clouds obſcure,
Would blinde mine eies,they might not ſee,
Thoſe cruell pleaſant lamps that lure:
My reaſon faine would ſet me free,
　　　　　　　Which may not be.

The dried ſtrawe will take the fire;
The trained brache will follow game:
The idle thought doth ſtill deſire:
Fond will is hardly brought in frame:
　　　　　　　The more my blame.

Thus ſee I how the ſtormes doe growe,
And yet the paine I ſtill approoue:
I leaue my weale,I follow woe,
I ſee the rocke,yet nill remooue:
　　　　　　　Oh flie me Loue:

Then midſt the ſtormes I ſhall preuent,
And by foreſight my troubles ceaſe:
And by my reaſon ſhun repent;
Thus ſhall I ioye,if Loue decreaſe:
　　　　　　　And liue in peace.

　　　　　T. L. Gent.
　　　H 2　　　　　　　My

MY fraile and earthly barke by reaſons guide,
(Which holds the helme, whilſt will doth yeld the
By my deſires the windes of bad betide,   (ſaile)
Hath ſaild theſe worldly ſeas with ſmall auaile,
Vaine obiects ſerue for dreadfull rocks to quaile,
 My brittle boate, from hauen of life that flies,
 To haunt the Sea of Mundane miſeries.

My ſoule that drawes impreſſions from aboue,
And viewes my courſe, and ſees the windes aſpire,
Bids reaſon watch to ſcape the ſhoales of Loue,
But lawles will enflamde with endles ire,
Doth ſteere in poope whilſt reaſon doth retire :
 The ſtorms increaſe, my barke loues billowes fill;
 Thus are they wrackt, that guide their courſe by will.

      T. L. Gent.

MIdſt laſting griefes, to haue but ſhort repoſe,
In little eaſe, to feede on loath'd ſuſpect,
Through deepe deſpite, aſſured loue to loſe,
In ſhew to like, in ſubſtance to neglect :

To laugh an howre, to weepe an age of woe,
From true miſhap to gather falſe delight,
To freeze in feare, in inward hart to glowe :
To read my loſſe within a ruthles ſight :

To ſeeke my weale, and wot not where it lies,
In hidden fraud, an open wrong to finde,
Of ancient thoughts, new fables to deuiſe,
Delightfull ſmiles, but yet a ſcornfull minde t

 These are the meanes that murder my releefe,
 And end my doubtfull hope with certaine greefe.

      T. L. Gent.

         Oh

OH woods vnto your walks my bodie hies,
To loofe the traitrous bonds of ticing Loue,
   Where trees,where herbes,where flowres,
   Their natiue moifture powres,
From foorth their tender ftalks to helpe mine eies,
Yet their vnited teares may nothing moue.

When I beheld the faire adorned tree,
Which lightnings force and winters frofts refifts,
   Then Daphnes ill betide,
   And Phebus lawles pride,
Enforce me fay euen fuch my forrowes be,
For felfe difdaine in Phebes hart confifts.

If I behold the flowres by morning teares,
Looke louely fweete,ah then forlorne I crie :
   Sweete fhowres for Memnon fhed,
   All flowres by you are fed :
Whereas my pitious plaint that ftill appeares,
Yeelds vigor to hir fcornes and makes me die.

When I regard the pretie greeffull burd,
With tearfull (yet delightfull)notes complaine,
   I yeeld a tenor with my teares,
   And whilft hir muficke wounds mine eares,
Alas fay I, why nill my notes affoord
Such like remorce,who ftill beweepe my paine.

When I behold vpon the leaueles bow,
The haples bird lament hir Loues depart,
   I drawe hir biding nigh,
   And fitting downe I figh,
And fighing fay alas,that birds auow
A fetled faith,where Phebe fcornes my fmart.

Thus wearie in my walks,and woefull too,
I fpend the day forefpent with daily griefe :
Each

Each obiect of diſtreſſe,
My ſorrow doth expreſſe :
I doate on that which doth my hart vndoe,
And honor hir that ſcornes to yeeld reliefe.

T. L. Gent.

ACcurſt be loue and they that truſt his train es
He taſtes the fruite,whilſt others toyle :
He brings the lampe,we lend the oyle :
He ſowes diſtres,we yeeld him ſoyle:
He wageth warre,we bide the foyle :

Accurſt be Loue,and thoſe that truſt his traines :
He laies the trap,we ſeeke the ſnare :
He threatneth death, we ſpeake him faire :
He coynes deceits,we foſter care :
He fauoreth pride,we count it rare.

Accurſt be Loue,and thoſe that truſt his traines,
He ſeemeth blinde,yet wounds with Art :
He vowes content,he paies with ſmart :
He ſweares reliefe,yet kils the hart :
He cals for truth,yet ſcornes deſart.
Accurſt be loue,and thoſe that truſt his traines,
Whoſe heauen,is hell ; whoſe perfect ioyes,are paines.

T. L. Gent.

NOw I finde,thy lookes were fained,
Quickly loſt,and quicklie gained :
Softe thy skin,like wooll of Wethers,
Hart vnſtable, light as feathers :
Toong vntruſtie,ſubtill ſighted :
Wanton will with change delighted,
Sirene pleaſant, foe to reaſon :
Cupid plague thee,for this treaſon.

Of

Of thine eies I made my myrror;
From thy beautie came mine error :
All thy words I counted wittie :
All thy ſmyles I deemed pittie :
Thy falſe teares that me agreeued,
Firſt of all my truſt deceiued.
　　Sirene pleaſant, &c.

Fain'd acceptance when I asked,
Louely words with cunning masked;
Holie vowes, but hart vnholie :
Wretched man my truſt was follie :
Lillie white, and pretie wincking,
Solemne vowes, but ſorie thinking.
　　Sirene pleaſant, &c.

Now I ſee, O ſeemely cruell,
Others warme them at my fuell :
Wit ſhall guide me in this durance,
Since in Loue is no aſſurance :
Change thy paſture, take thy pleaſure,
Beautie is a fading treaſure,
　　Sirene pleaſant, &c.

Prime youth laſts not, age will follow,
And make white theſe treſſes yelow :
Wrinckled face, for lookes delightfull,
Shall acquaint the dame deſpitefull :
And when time ſhall date thy glorie,
Then too late thou wilt be ſorie.
　　Sirene pleaſant, &c.
　　　　　　　　　T. L. Gent.

THe fatall ſtarre that at my birthday ſhined,
Were it of Ioue, or Venus in hir brightnes,
All ſad effects, ſowre fruits of loue diuined,
　　　　　In my Loues lightnes,

　　　　　　　　　　　　Light

Light was my Loue, that all too light beleeued :
Heauens ruthe to dwell in faire alluring faces,
That loue, that hope, that damned, and repreeued,
    To all diſgraces.

Loue that miſled, hope that deceiu'd my ſeeing :
Loue hope no more, mockt with deluding obiect :
Sight full of ſorow, that denies the being,
    Vnto the ſubiect.

Soul leaue the ſeat, wher thoughts with endles ſwelling,
Change into teares and words of no perſuaſion :
Teares turne to tongs, and ſpend your tunes in telling,
    Sorowes inuaſion.

Wonder vaine world at beauties proud refuſall :
Wonder in vaine at Loues vnkinde deniall,
Why Loue thus loftie is, that doth abuſe all :
    And makes no triall.

Teares, words, and tunes, all ſignifie my ſadnes :
My ſpeechles griefe, looke pale without diſſembling :
Sorow ſit mute, and tell thy torments madnes,
    With true harts trembling.

And if pure vowes, or hands heau'd vp to heauen,
May moue the Gods to rue my wretched blindnes,
My plaints ſhall make my ioyes in meaſure euen,
    With hir vnkindnes.

That ſhe whom my true hart hath found ſo cruell,
Mourning all mirthles may purſue the pleaſure,
That ſcornes hir labors : poore in hir ioyes iewell,
    And earthly treaſure.

     T. L. Gent.

       Faine

FAine to content, I bend my ſelfe to write,
But what to write,my minde can ſcarce conceiue :
Your radiant eies craue obiects of delight,
My hart no glad impreſſions can receiue :
    To write of griefe,is but a tedious thing :
    And wofull men,of woe muſt needly ſing.

To write the truce,the wars,the ſtrife,the peace,
That Loue once wrought in my diſtempred hart :
Were but to cauſe my woonted woes encreaſe,
And yeeld new life to my concealed ſmart :
    Who tempts the eare with tedious lines of griefe,
    That waits for ioy, complaines without reliefe.

To write what paines ſupplanteth others ioy,
For-thy is folly in the greateſt wit,
Who feeles,may beſt decipher the annoy,
Who knowes the griefe, but he that taſteth it ?
    Who writes of woe, muſt needes be woe begone,
    And writing feele,and feeling write of mone.

To write the temper of my laſt deſire,
That likes me beſt,and appertains you moſt :
You are the Pharos whereto now retire,
My thoughts long wandring in a forren coaſt,
    In you they liue,to other ioyes they die,
    And liuing draw their foode from your faire eie.

Enforſt by Loue,and that effectuall fire,
That ſprings from you to quicken loiall harts :
I write in part the prime of my deſire,
My faith,my feare, that ſprings from your deſarts ;
    My faith,whoſe firmnes neuer ſhunneth triall,
    My feare,the dread and danger of deniall.

To write in briefe, a legend in a line,
My hart hath vow'd to draw his life from yours ;

I   My

My lookes haue made a Sunne of your ſweete eine,
My ſoule doth drawe his eſſence from your powres :
   And what I am, in fortune or in loue,
   All thoſe haue ſworne, to ſerue for your behoue.

My ſences ſucke their comforts from your ſweete,
My inward minde, your outward faire admires ;
My hope lies proſtrate at your pities feete,
My hart, lookes, ſoule, ſence, minde, and hope deſires ;
   Beleefe, and fauour, in your louely ſight,
   Els all will ceaſe to liue, and pen to write.

T. L. Gent.

FVll fraught with vnrecomptles ſweete,
Of your faire face that ſtole mine eie,
No gladſome day my lookes did greete,
Wherein I wiſht not willingly ;
   Mine eies were ſhut I might not ſee,
   A Ladie of leſſe maieſtie.

What moſt I like, I neuer minde,
And ſo on you haue fixt my thoughts,
That others ſights doe make me blinde,
And what I ſee but you is noughts ;
   By vſe and cuſtome thus you ſee,
   Another nature liues in mee.

The more I looke, the more I loue,
The more I thinke, the more I thriue,
No obieɛt can my looke remoue,
No thought can better thoughts reuiue,
   For what I ſee or thinke, I finde,
   Exceedeth ſight or thought of minde.

Since then your lookes, haue ſtolne mine eies,
And eies content to nouriſh loue,

                       And

And loue doth make my thoughts ariſe,
And thoughts are firme, and will not moue,
Vouchſafe to knit by powre vnknowne,
Our eies, our loues, our thoughts in one.

T. L. Gent.

Ike deſart woods, with darkſome ſhades obſcured,
Where dredful beaſts, wher hateful horror raigneth
Such is my wounded hart whom ſorrow paineth.

The trees, are fatall ſhafts, to death inured,
That cruell Loue within my breaſt maintaineth,
To whet my griefe, when as my ſorrow waineth.

The gaſtly beaſts, my thoughts in cares aſſured,
Which wage me warre, whilſt hart no ſuccor gaineth,
With falſe ſuſpect, and feare that ſtill remaineth.

The horrors, burning ſighes by cares procured,
Which forth I ſend, whilſt weeping eie complaineth,
To coole the heate, the helples hart containeth.

But ſhafts, but cares, ſighes, horrors vnrecured,
Were nought eſteemde, if for theſe paines awarded,
My faithfull Loue by you might be rewarded.

T. L. Gent.

Or pittie pretie eies ſurceaſe,
To giue me warre, and graunt me peace,
Triumphant eies, why beare you Armes,
Againſt a hart that thinks no harmes.
A hart alreadie quite appalde,
A hart that yeelds, and is enthrald,
Kill Rebels prowdly that reſiſt,
Not thoſe that in true faith perſiſt.

I 2   And

And conquered ſerue your Deitie,
Will you alas commaund me die ?
Then die I yours ,and death my croſſe,
But vnto you pertains the loſſe.

T. L. Gent.

MY bonie Laſſe thine eie,
            So ſlie,
Hath made me ſorrowe ſo :
Thy Crimſen cheekes my deere,
            So cleere,
Haue ſo much wrought my woe.

Thy pleaſing ſmiles and grace,
            Thy face,
Haue rauiſht ſo my ſprights :
That life is growne to nought,
            Through thought,
Of Loue which me affrights.

For fancies flames of fire,
            Aſpire,
Vnto ſuch furious powre :
As but the teares I ſhead,
            Make dead,
The brands would me deuoure.

I ſhould conſume to nought,
            Through thought,
Of thy faire ſhining eie :
Thy cheekes,thy pleaſing ſmiles,
            The wiles,
That forſt my hart to die.

Thy grace,thy face,the part,
            Where art,

Stands

Stands gazing ſtill to ſee :
The wondrous gifts and powre,
                    Each howre,
That hath bewitched me.

T. L. Gent.

ALas my hart, mine eie hath wronged thee,
Preſumptious eie, to gaze on Phillis face :
Whoſe heauenly eie, no mortall man my ſee,
But he muſt die, or purchaſe Phillis grace ;   (thee,
    Poore Coridon, the Nimph whoſe eie doth moue
    Doth loue to draw, but is not drawne to loue thee.

Hir beautie, Natures pride, and Shepherds praiſe,
Hir eie, the heauenly Planet of my life,
Hir matchles wit, and grace, hir fame diſplaies,
As if that Ioue had made hir for his wife ;
    Onely hir eies ſhoote firie darts to kill,
    Yet is hir hart, as cold as Caucaſe hill.

My wings too weake, to flie againſt the Sunne,
Mine eies vnable to ſuſtaine hir light,
My hart doth yeeld, that I am quite vndoon,
Thus hath faire Phillis ſlaine me with hir ſight :
    My bud is blaſted, withered is my leafe,
    And all my corne is rotted in the ſheafe.

Phillis, the golden fetter of my minde,
My fancies Idoll, and my vitall powre ;
Goddeſſe of Nimphes, and honor of thy kinde,
This Ages Phenix, Beauties braueſt bowre ;
    Poore Coridon for loue of thee muſt die,
    Thy Beauties thrall, and conqueſt of thine eie.

Leaue Coridon, to plough the barren feeld,
Thy buds of hope are blaſted with diſgrace ;

For

For Phillis lookes,no hartie loue doe yeeld,
Nor can fhe loue,for all hir louely face,
   Die Coridon,the fpoyle of Phillis eie,
   She can not loue,and therefore thou muft die.

VVHat cunnnig can expreffe
   The fauor of hir face,
To whom in this diftreffe,
I doe appeale for grace,
   A thoufand Cupids flie,
   About hir gentle eie.

From whence each throwes a dart,
That kindleth foft fweete fier :
Within my fighing hart,
Poffeffed by defier :
   No fweeter life I trie,
   Than in hir loue to die.

The Lillie in the fielde,
That glories in his white :
For purenes now muft yeelde,
And render vp his right :
   Heau'n pictur'de in hir face,
   Doth promife ioy and grace.

Faire Cinthias filuer light,
That beates on running ftreames ;
Compares not with hir white,
Whofe haires are all funbeames ;
   Hir vertues fo doe fhine,
   As daie vnto mine eine.

With this there is a Red,
Exceeds the Damaske Rofe ;
Which in hir cheekes is fpred ;

Whence

Whence euery fauor groes,
    In skie there is no ſtarre,
    That ſhe ſurmounts not farre.

When Phœbus from the bed,
Of Thetis doth ariſe,
The morning bluſhing red,
In faire carnation wiſe,
    He ſhewes it in hir face,
    As Queene of euery grace.

This pleaſant Lillie white,
This taint of roſeat red,
This Cinthias ſiluer light,
This ſweete faire Dea ſpread,
    Theſe ſunbeames in mine eie,
    Theſe beauties make me die.

E. O.

A moſt excellent paſſion ſet downe
by *N. B. Gent.*

COm yonglings com, that ſeem to make ſuch mone,
  About a thing of nothing God he knowes :
With ſighes and ſobs, and many a greeuous grone,
And trickling teares, that ſecret ſorow ſhowes,
    Leaue, leaue to faine, and here behold indeed,
    The onely man, may make your harts to bleed.

Whoſe ſtate to tell ; no, neuer toong can tell :
Whoſe woes are ſuch ; oh no, there are none ſuch :
Whoſe hap ſo hard : nay rather halfe a hell :
Whoſe griefe ſo much : yea God he knowes too much :
    Whoſe wofull ſtate, and greeuous hap (alas,)
    The world may ſee, is ſuch as neuer was.
                        Good

Good nature weepes to ſee hir ſelfe abuſed;
Ill fortune ſhewes hir furie in hir face :
Poore reaſon pines to ſee hir ſelfe refuſed :
And dutie dies, to ſee his ſore diſgrace.
     Hope hangs the head, to ſee diſpaire ſo neere ;
     And what but death can end this heauie cheere ?

Oh curſed cares, that neuer can be knowne :
Dole, worſe than death, when neuer tong can tell it :
The hurt is hid, although the ſorow ſhowne,
Such is my paine, no pleaſure can expell it.
     In ſumme I ſee, I am ordained I :
     To liue in dole, and ſo in ſorow die.

Behold each teare, no token of a toy :
But torments ſuch, as teare my hart aſunder :
Each ſobbing ſigh, a ſigne of ſuch annoy,
That how I liue, beleeue me 'tis a wonder.
     Each grone, a gripe, that makes me gaſpe for breath:
     And euerie ſtraine, a bitter pang of death.

Loe thus I liue, but looking ſtill to die :
And ſtill I looke, but ſtill I ſee in vaine :
And ſtill in vaine, alas, I lie and crie :
And ſtill I crie, but haue no eaſe of paine.
     So ſtill in paine, I liue, looke, lie, and crie :
     When hope would helpe, or death would let me die.

Sometime I ſleepe, a ſlumber, not a ſleepe :
And then I dreame (God knowes) of no delight,
But of ſuch woes, as makes me lie and weepe
Vntill I wake, in ſuch a pitious plight ;
     As who beheld me ſleeping or awaking,
     Would ſay my hart were in a heauie taking.

Looke as the dew doth lie vpon the ground,
So ſits the ſweate of ſorow on my face :

                             Oh

Oh deadly dart,that ſtrooke ſo deepe a wound,
Oh hatefull hap,to hit in ſuch a place :
　　The hart is hurt,and bleedes the bodie ouer :
　　Yet cannot die,nor euer health recouer.

Then he or ſhe,that hath a happie hand,
To helpe a hart,that hath no hope to liue :
Come,come with ſpeede,and do not ſtaying ſtand :
But if no one,can any comfort giue,
　　Run to the Church, and bid the Sexton toule
　　A ſolemne knell,yet for a ſilie ſoule.

Harke how it ſounds,that ſorrow laſteth long :
Long,long : long long : long long,and longer yet :
Oh cruell death : thou dooſt me double wrong,
To let me lie ſo long in ſuch a fit :
　　Yet when I die,write neighbors where I lie;
　　Long was I dead,ere death would let me die.

THeſe lines I ſend by waues of woe,
　　And bale becomes my boate :
Which ſighes of ſorowes ſtill ſhall keepe,
　　On floods of feare afloate.

My ſighes ſhall ſerue me ſtill for winde,
　　My lading is my ſmart :
And true report my pilot is,
　　My hauen is thy hart.

My keele is fram'd of crabbed care,
　　My ribs are all of ruthe :
My planks are nothing elſe but plants,
　　With treenailes ioinde with truthe.

My maine maſt made of nought but mone,
　　My tackling trickling teares :
　　　　　　K　　　　　　　　　　And

And Topyard like a troubled minde,
    A flagge of follie beares.

My Cable is a conſtant hart,
    My Anckor luckles Loue :
Which Reaſons Capſtones from the ground,
    Of griefe can not remoue.

My Decks are all of deepe diſgrace,
    My Compas diſcontent;
And perill is my Northern Pole,
    And death my Orient.

My Saylers are my ſorowing thoughts,
    The Boateſwane bitter ſence:
The Maſter, miſerie; his mate
    Is dolefull diligence.
                    Sir W. H.

FEede ſtill thy ſelfe, thou fondling with beliefe,
  Go hunt thy hope, that neuer tooke effect,
Accuſe the wrongs that oft hath wrought thy griefe,
And reckon ſure where reaſon would ſuſpect.

Dwell in the dreames of wiſh and vaine deſire,
Purſue the faith that flies and ſeekes to new,
Run after hopes that mocke thee with retire,
And looke for loue where liking neuer grew.

Deuiſe conceits to eaſe thy carefull hart,
Truſt vpon times and daies of grace behinde,
Preſume the rights of promiſe and deſart,
And meaſure loue by thy beleeuing minde.

Force thy affects that ſpite doth daily chace,
Winke at the wrongs with wilfull ouerſight,

                                     See

See not the ſoyle and ſtaine of thy diſgrace,
Nor recke diſdaine, to doate on thy delite.

And when thou ſeeſt the end of thy reward,
And theſe effects enſue of thine aſſault,
When raſhnes rues, that reaſon ſhould regard,
Yet ſtill accuſe thy fortune for the fault.
    And crie, O Loue, O death, O vaine deſire,
    When thou complainſt the heate, & feeds the fire.

MY firſt borne loue vnhappily conceiued,
  Brought foorth in paine, & chriſtened with a curſe
Die in your Infancie, of life bereaued,
        By your cruell nurſe.

Reſtleſſe deſire, from my Loue that proceeded,
Leaue to be, and ſeeke your heauen by dieng,
Since you, O you ? your owne hope haue exceeded,
        By too hie flieng.

And you my words, my harts faithfull expounders,
No more offer your Iewell, vneſteemed,
Since thoſe eies my Loues life and liues confounders,
        Your woorth miſdeemed.

Loue leaue to deſire, words leaue it to vtter,
Swell on my thoughts, till you breake that contains you
My complaints in thoſe deafe eares no more mutter,
        That ſo diſdaines you.

And you careles of me, that without feeling,
With drie eies, behold my Tragedie ſmiling,   (yeelding
Decke your proude triumphes with your poore ſlaues
        To his owne ſpoyling.

But if that wrong, or holy truth diſpiſed,
To iuſt reuenge, the heauens euer moued,

So let hir loue,and ſo be ſtill denied,
　　Who ſhe ſo loued.

THe brainſicke race that wanton youth enſues,
　Without regard to grounded wiſdomes lore,
As often as I thinke thereon,renues
The freſh remembrance of an ancient ſore :
　　Reuoking to my penſiue thoughts at laſt,
　　The worlds of wickednes that I haue paſt.

And though experience bids me bite on bit,
And champe the bridle of a better ſmacke,
Yet coſtly is the price of after wit,
Which brings ſo cold repentance at hir backe :
　　And skill that's with ſo many loſſes bought,
　　Men ſay is little better worth than nought.

And yet this fruit I muſt confeſſe doth growe
Of follies ſcourge : that though I now complaine
Of error paſt,yet henceforth I may knowe
To ſhun the whip that threats the like againe :
　　For wiſe men though they ſmart a while,had leuer
　　To learne experience at the laſt,than neuer.

THoſe eies which ſet my fancie on a fire,
　Thoſe criſped haires,which hold my hart in chains,
Thoſe daintie hands,which conquer'd my deſire,
That wit,which of my thoughts doth hold the rains.

Thoſe eies for cleernes doe the ſtarrs ſurpas,
Thoſe haires obſcure the brightnes of the Sunne,
Thoſe hands more white, than euer Iuorie was,
That wit euen to the skies hath glorie woon.

O eies that pearce our harts without remorſe,
O haires of right that weares a roiall crowne,

O

O hands that conquer more than Cæſars force,
O wit that turns huge kingdoms vpſide downe.

Then Loue be Iudge,what hart may thee withſtand :
Such eies,ſuch haire,ſuch wit, and ſuch a hand.

PRaiſd be Dianas faire and harmles light,
Praiſd be the dewes,wherwith ſhe moiſts the ground;
Praiſd be hir beames, the glorie of the night,
Praiſd be hir powre,by which all powres abound.

Praiſd be hir Nimphs,with whom ſhe decks the woods,
Praiſd be hir knights, in whom true honor liues,
Praiſd be that force,by which ſhe moues the floods,
Let that Diana ſhine,which all theſe giues.

In heauen Queene ſhe is among the ſpheares,
In ay ſhe Miſtres like makes all things pure,
Eternitie in hir oft chaunge ſhe beares,
She beautie is,by hir the faire endure.

Time weares hir not,ſhe doth his chariot guide,
Mortalitie belowe hir orbe is plaſte,
By hir the vertue of the ſtarrs downe ſlide,
In hir is vertues perfect image caſt.

A knowledge pure it is hir worth to kno,
With Circes let them dwell that thinke not ſo.

LIke to a Hermite poore in place obſcure,
I meane to ſpend my daies of endles doubt,
To waile ſuch woes as time cannot recure,
Where none but Loue ſhall euer finde me out.

My foode ſhall be of care and ſorow made,
My drink noughtelſe but teares falne from mine eies,
                                        And

And for my light in such obscured shade,
The flames shall serue, which from my hart arise.

A gowne of graie, my bodie shall attire,
My staffe of broken hope whereon Ile staie,
Of late repentance linckt with long desire,
The couch is fram'de whereon my limbes Ile lay,

And at my gate dispaire shall linger still,
To let in death when Loue and Fortune will.

Like truthles dreames, so are my ioyes expired,
And past returne, are all my dandled daies :
My loue misled, and fancie quite retired,
Of all which past, the sorow onely staies.

My lost delights, now cleane from sight of land,
Haue left me all alone in vnknowne waies :
My minde to woe, my life in fortunes hand,
Of all which past, the sorow onely staies.

As in a countrey strange without companion,
I onely waile the wrong of deaths delaies,
Whose sweete spring spent, whose sommer wel nie don,
Of all which past, the sorow onely staies.

Whom care forewarnes, ere age and winter colde,
To haste me hence, to finde my fortunes folde.

A Secret murder hath bene done of late,
Vnkindnes founde, to be the bloudie knife,
And shee that did the deede a dame of state,
Faire, gracious, wise, as any beareth life.

To quite hir selfe, this answere did she make,
Mistrust (quoth she) hath brought him to his end,

Which

Which makes the man ſo much himſelfe miſtake,
To lay the guilt vnto his guiltles frend.

Ladie not ſo,not feard I found my death,
For no deſart thus murdered is my minde,
And yet before I yeeld my fainting breath,
I quite the killer,tho I blame the kinde.

    You kill vnkinde,I die, and yet am true,
    For at your ſight, my wound doth bleede anew.

SOught by the world,and hath the world diſdain'd,
Is ſhe, my hart,for whom thou dooſt endure,
Vnto whoſe grace,ſith Kings haue not obtaind,
Sweete is thy choiſe,though loſſe of life be ſowre :
    Yet to the man,whoſe youth ſuch pains muſt proue,
    No better end,than that which comes by Loue.

Steere then thy courſe vnto the port of death,
Sith thy hard hap no betrer hap may finde,
Where when thou ſhalt vnlade thy lateſt breath,
Enuie hir ſelfe ſhall ſwim to ſaue thy minde,
    Whoſe bodie ſunke in ſearch to gaine that ſhore,
    Where many a Prince had periſhed before.

And yet my hart it might haue been foreſeene,
Sith skilfull medcins mends each kinde of griefe,
Then in my breaſt full ſafely hadſt thou beene,
But thou my hart wouldſt neuer me beleeue,
    Who tolde thee true,when firſt thou didſt aſpire,
    Death was the end of euery ſuch deſire.

HIr face,	Hir tong,	Hir wit,
So faire,	So ſweete,	So ſharpe,
Firſt bent,	Then drew,	Then hit,
Mine eie,	Mine eare,	My hart.

                        Mine

Mine eie,	Mine eare,	My hart,
To like,	To learne,	To loue,
Hir face,	Hir tong,	Hir wit,
Doth lead,	doth teach,	Doth moue.
Oh face,	Oh tong,	Oh wit,
With frownes,	With checke,	With smart,
Wrong not,	Vexe not,	Wound not,
Mine eie,	Mine eare,	My hart.
Mine eie,	Mine eare,	My hart,
To learne,	To knowe,	To feare,
Hir face,	Hir tong,	Hir wit,
Doth lead,	Doth teach,	Doth sweare.

CAlling to minde mine eie long went about,
T'entice my hart to seeke to leaue my brest,
All in a rage I thought to pull it out,
By whose deuice I liu'd in such vnrest,
    What could it say to purchase so my grace ?
    Forsooth that it had seene my Mistres face.

Another time I likewise call to minde,
My hart was he that all my woe had wrought,
For he my brest the fort of Loue resignde,
When of such warrs my fancie neuer thought,
    What could it say, when I would him haue slaine ?
    But he was yours, and had forgone me cleane.

At length when I perceiu'd both eie and hart,
Excusde themselues, as guiltles of mine ill,
I found my selfe was cause of all my smart,
And tolde my selfe, my selfe now slay I will :
    But when I found my selfe to you was true,
    I lou'd my selfe, bicause my selfe lou'd you.

                  What

WHat elſe is hell, but loſſe of blisfull heauen?
    What darknes elſe, but lacke of lightſome day?
What elſe is death, but things of life bereauen?
What winter elſe, but pleaſant ſprings decay?

Vnreſt what elſe, but fancies hot deſire,
Fed with delay, and followed with diſpaire?
What elſe miſhap, but longing to aſpire,
To ſtriue againſt, earth, water, fire and aire?

Heauen were my ſtate, and happie Sunneſhine day,
And life moſt bleſt, to ioy one howres deſire,
Hap, bliſſe, and reſt, and ſweete ſpringtime of May,
Were to behold my faire conſuming fire.

But loe, I feele, by abſence from your ſight,
Miſhap, vnreſt, death, winter, hell, darke night.

WOuld I were chaung'd into that golden ſhowre,
    That ſo diuinely ſtreamed from the skies,
To fall in drops vpon the daintie floore,
Where in hir bed, ſhe ſolitarie lies,
    Then would I hope ſuch ſhowres as richly ſhine,
    Would pearce more deepe than theſe waſt teares of
                                                    (mine.
Or would I were that plumed Swan, ſnowe white,
Vnder whoſe forme, was hidden heauenly power,
Then in that riuer would I moſt delite,
Whoſe waues doe beate, againſt hir ſtately bower,
    And in thoſe banks, ſo tune my dying ſong,
    That hir deafe ears, would think my plaint too long.

Elſe would I were, Narciſſus, that ſweete boy,
And ſhe hir ſelfe, the ſacred fountaine cleere,
Who rauiſht with the pride of his owne ioy,
Drenched his lims, with gazing ouer neere:
                                L   So

So should I bring, my soule to happie rest,
To end my life, in that I loued best.

WHo plucks thee down frō hie desire poor hart? **Care.**
Who comforts thee in depth of thy distresse ? **Care.**
Amid contents, who breeds thy secret smart ? **Care.**
Who seekes the meane, thy sorrowes may be lesse ? **Care.**

Who calls thy wits togither to their worke ? **Care.**
Who warnes thy will, to follow warie wit ? **Care.**
Who lets thee see in loue what sorrowes lurke ? **Care.**
Who makes thee feele the force of fancies fit ? **Care.**

Who taught thee first to trie before thou trust ? **Care.**
Who bids thee keepe a faithfull tried freend ? **Care.**
Who wils thee say, loue wantons he that lust ? **Care.**
Who winnes the wish, that hath a happie end ? **Care.**

Care then to keepe, that faithfull friend in store,
Whose loue commands, that thou shalt care no more.

THose eies that holds the hand of euery hart,
Those hands that holds the hart of euery eie,
That wit that goes beyond all natures Art,
That sence too deepe, for wisdome to discrie,
That eie, that hand, that wit, that heauenly sence,
All these doth show my Mistres Excellence.

Oh eies that perce into the purest hart,
Oh hands that hold, the highest harts in thrall,
Oh wit that weyes the deapth of all desart,
Oh sence that showes, the secret sweete of all,   (thee,
The heauen of heuens, with heuenly powrs preserue
Loue but thy selfe, and giue me leaue to serue thee.

To serue, to liue, to looke vpon those eies,
To looke, to liue, to kisse that heauenlie hand,

To

To ſound that wit,that doth amaze the wiſe,
To know that ſence,no ſence can vnderſtand,
　　To vnderſtande that all the world may know,
　　Such wit,ſuch ſence,eies,hands,there are no moe.

WHo liſt to heare the ſum of ſorrowes ſtate,
　　The depth of dole,wherein a minde may dwell,
The loathed life,that happie harts may hate,
The ſaddeſt tale,that euer toong could tell,
　　But reade this verſe,and ſay who wrote the ſame,
　　Doth onely dwell,where comfort neuer came.

A carefull head,firſt croſt with crooked hap,
A wofull wit,bewitcht with wretched will,
A clyming hart,falne downe from Fortunes lap,
A bodie borne,to looſe his labour ſtill,
　　A mourning minde,ſore mated with deſpite,
　　May ſerue to ſhewe,the lacke of my delite.

Yet more than this,a hope ſtill founde in vaine,
A vile diſpaire,that ſpeakes but of diſtreſſe,
A forſt content,to ſuffer deadly paine,
A paine ſo great,as can not get redreſſe,
　　Will all affirme,my ſum of ſorrow ſuch,
　　As neuer man,that euer knew ſo much.

AS rare to heare,as ſeldome to be ſeene,
　　It can not be,nor euer yet hath beene,
That fire ſhould burne,with perfect heate and flame,
Without ſome matter for to yeeld the ſame.

A ſtraunger caſe,yet true by proofe I knowe,
A man in ioye,that liued ſtill in woe,
Burnt with deſire,and doth poſſe at will,
Enioying all,yet all deſiring ſtill.
　　　　　　　　　　L 2　　　　　Who

Who hath ynough,yet thinks he liues without,
To want no loue,and yet to ſtand in doubt,
What diſcontent,to liue in ſuch deſire,
To haue his will,yet euer to require.

THe time,when firſt I fell in Loue,
    Which now I muſt lament,
The yeere, wherein I loſt ſuch time,
    to compaſſe my content.

The day,wherein I ſawe too late,
    The follies of a Louer,
The hower,wherein I found ſuch loſſe,
    As care cannot recouer.

And laſt,the minute of miſhap,
    Which makes me thus to plaine,
The dolefull fruits of Louers ſutes,
    Which labor loſe in vaine :

Doth make me ſolemnly proteſt,
    As I with paine doe proue,
There is no time,yeere,day,nor howre,
    Nor minute,good to loue.

WHen day is gone,and darknes come,
    The toyling tired wight,
Doth vſe to eaſe his wearie bones,
    By reſt in quiet night.

When ſtorme is ſtaied,and harbor woon,
    The Sea man ſet on ſhore,
With comfort doth requite the care,
    Of perils paſt before.

                        When

When Loue hath woon,where it did woo,
    And light where it delites,
Contented minde,thenceforth forgets,
    The frowne of former ſpites.

THough neither tears nor torments can be thought,
    Nor death it ſelfe too deere to be ſuſtaind,
To win thoſe ioyes ſo woorthie to be ſought,
So rare to reach,ſo ſweete to be obtaind.

Yet earneſt Loue,with longing to aſpire,
To that which hope holds in ſo high regarde,
Makes time delaid,a torment to deſire,
When Loue with hope forbeares his iuſt rewarde.

    Then bleſſed hope haſte on thy happie daies,
    Saue my deſire,by ſhortning thy delaies.

A notable deſcription of the World.

OF thick and thin,light,heauie,dark and cleere,   Mixtures.
    White,black,& blew,red,green,& purple die: Coulors.
Gold,Siluer,Braſſe,Lead,Iron,Tin, and Copper,   Mettals.
Moiſt aire,hot fire, cold water, earth full drie :   Elements:
Blood,Choler,Flegme,and Melancholie by,   Cóplexiós.
A mixed maſſe,a Chaos all confuſde,   Chaos.
Such was the world,till God diuiſion vſde.

In framing heau'n and earth,God did diuide,
The firſt daies light,and darkth,to night and day.   1
The ſecond,he a firmament applide,   2
Third,fruitfull earth appeerd,Seas tooke their way,   3
Fourth,Sun and Moone, with Stars in skies he fixt,   4
Fift,Fiſh and Foule,the Sea and land poſſeſt,   5
And God made Man,like to himſelfe,the ſixt :   6
                           The

7 The ſeauenth day, when all things he had bleſt :
He hallowed that, and therein tooke his reſt.

W. S. Gent.

BY wracke late driuen on ſhoare, from Cupids Crare,
Whoſe ſailes of error, ſighes of hope and feare,
Conueied through ſeas of teares, and ſands of care,
Till rocks of high diſdaine, hir ſides did teare,
 I write a dirge, for dolefull doues to ſing,
 With ſelfe ſame quill, I pluckt from Cupids wing.

Farewell vnkinde, by whom I fare ſo ill,
Whoſe looks bewitcht my thoughts with falſe ſurmiſe,
Till forced reaſon did vnbinde my will,
And ſhewed my hart, the follie of mine eies,
 And ſaide, attending where I ſhould attaine,
 Twixt wiſh and want, was but a pleaſing paine.

Farewell vnkinde, my floate is at an ebbe,
My troubled thoughts, are turnd to quiet wars,
My fancies hope hath ſpun and ſpent hir webbe,
My former wounds, are cloſed vp with skars,
 As aſhes lie, longe ſince conſumde with fire,
 So is my loue, ſo now is my deſire.

Farewell vnkinde, my firſt and finall loue,
Whoſe coie contempts, it bootes not heere to name,
But gods are iuſt, and euery ſtar aboue,
Doth threat reuenge, where faith's reward is blame,
 And I may liue, though your deſpiſed thrall,
 By fond miſchoyce, to ſee your fortunes fall.

Farewell vnkinde, moſt cruell of your kinde,
By whom my worth, is drowned in diſdaines,
As was my loue, ſo is your iudgement blinde,
My fortune ill, and ſuch hath bene my gaines,

        But

But this for all, I liſt no more to ſaie,
Farewell faire proude, not lifes, but loues decaie.

THe gentle ſeaſon of the yeere,
　Hath made my bloming branch appeere,
　　And beautified the land with flowres,
The aire doth ſauor with delight,
The heauens doe ſmile, to ſee the ſight,
　　And yet mine eies, augments their ſhowres.

The meades are mantled all with greene,
The trembling leaues, haue cloth'd the treene,
　　The birds with feathers new doe ſing,
But I poore ſoule, when wrong doth wrack,
Attyres my ſelfe in mourning black,
　　Whoſe leafe doth fall amid his ſpring.

And as you ſee the skarlet Roſe,
In his ſweete prime, his buds diſcloſe,
　　Whoſe hewe is with the Sun reuiued,
So in the Aprill of mine age,
My liuely colours doe aſſwage,
　　Becauſe my Sun-ſhine is depriued.

My hart that wonted was of yore,
Light as the winde abroad to ſore,
　　Amongſt the buds when beautie ſprings,
Now onely houers ouer you,
As doth the birde thats taken new,
　　And mourns when all hir neighbours ſings.

When euery man is bent to ſport,
Then penſiue I alone reſort,
　　Into ſome ſolitarie walke,
As doth the dolefull Turtle doue,
Who hauing loſt hir faithfull loue,
　　Sits mourning on ſome withered ſtalke.

　　　　　　　　　　　There

There to my ſelfe, I doe recount,
How far my woes, my ioyes ſurmount,
    How Loue requiteth me with hate :
How all my pleaſures end in paine,
How hate doth ſay, my hope is vaine,
    How fortune frownes vpon my ſtate.

And in this moode, charg'd with deſpaire,
With vapored ſighes, I dim the aire,
    And to the Gods make this requeſt :
That by the ending of my life,
I may haue truce with this ſtrange ſtrife,
    And bring my ſoule to better reſt.

A Counterloue.

DEclare O minde, from fond deſires excluded,
    That thou didſt find erewhile, by Loue deluded.

An eie, the plot, whereon Loue ſets his gin,
Beautie, the trap, wherein the heedles fall,
A ſmile, the traine, that drawes the ſimple in,
Sweete words, the wilie inſtrument of all,
    Intreaties poſts, faire promiſes are charmes,
    Writing, the meſſenger, that wooes our harmes.

Miſtreſſe, and ſeruant, titles of miſchaunce :
Commaundments done, the act of ſlauerie,
Their coulors worne, a clowniſh cogniſaunce,
And double dutie, pettie drudgerie,
    And when ſhe twines and dallies with thy locks,
    Thy freedome then is brought into the ſtocks.

To touch hir hand, hir hand bindes thy deſire,
To weare hir ring, hir ring is Neſſus gift,
To feele hir breſt, hir breſt doth blowe the fire,
To ſee hir bare, hir bare a balefull drift,

                                        To

To baite thine eies thereon,is loſſe of ſight,
To thinke of it,confounds thy ſenſes quite.

Kiſſes the keies,to ſweete conſuming ſin,
Cloſings, Cleopatras adders at thy breſt,
Fained reſiſtance then ſhe will begin,
And yet vnſatiable in all the reſt,
    And when thou dooſt vnto the act proceede,
    The bed doth grone,and tremble at the deede.

Beautie,a ſiluer dew that falls in May,
Loue is an Egſhell,with that humor fild,
Deſire,a winged boy,comming that way,
Delights and dallies with it in the field,
    The firie Sun, drawes vp the ſhell on hie,
    Beautie decaies,Loue dies,deſire doth flie.

    Vnharmd giue eare,that thing is hap'ly caught,
    That coſt ſome deere,if thou maiſt ha't for naught.

AS ioy of ioyes, and neuer dying blis,
Is to behold that mightie powre diuine,
Nor may we craue more bleſſednes than this,
With face to face,to ſee his glorie ſhine,
    So heere on earth,the onely good I finde
    Is your ſweete ſight, my whole content of minde.

If to the hart,mine eie doth truthe impart,
More faire of late,than erſt before you ſeeme,
Which beautie,though it breede my endles ſmart,
Yet ſtill I loue and worthily eſteeme,
    And if thoſe beames,would ſhine vpon me ſtill,
    Then had I heauen, and happines at will.

Some things by ſmelling liue,as fame report,
And ſome the water ioy,to their deſire,

      M   The

The subtile ayre,contents another sort,
And other some by taste and touch of fire,
   If snch can liue with things of small delight,
   Much more should I,enioying of your sight.

SEt me where Phœbus heate,the flowers slaieth,
Or where continuall snowe withstands his forces,
Set me where he his temprate raies displaieth,
Or where he comes,or where he neuer courses.

Set me in Fortunes grace,or else discharged,
In sweete and pleasant aire,or darke and glooming,
Where daies and nights,are lesser,or inlarged,
In yeeres of strength,in failing age,or blooming.

Set me in heauen,or earth,or in the center,
Lowe in a vale, or on a mountaine placed,
Set me to daunger,perill,and aduenture,
Graced by Fame,or infamie disgraced.

   Set me to these,or anie other triall,
   Except my Mistres anger and deniall.

I sawe the eies,that haue my seeing bounde,
I harde the toong,that made my speech to staie,
Hir wit,my thoughts did captiue and confounde,
And with hir graces,drew my life away,
   Vnto hir life,in whom my sences liues,
   My spirit vp himselfe,for tribute giues.

She sawe mine eies,and they recouer'd light,
She spake to me,and I had powre to speake,
She graced me,and I regained spright,
She freed my hart,that readie was to breake,
   My life,that erst beginning had in me,
   Now by hir being,doth begin to be.

                       Mine

Mine eies, behold the beautie raignes in hir,
Speake toong of hir, that nothing is but wonder,
To honor hir, my ſpirits onely ſtir,
Serue hir my hart, or hart deuide aſunder :
    And life, liue in the fauor ſhe hath ſhowne, (owne.
    Whereby thou haſt more ſtrength than was thine

    Miſtres, this grace, vnto your ſeruant giue,
    Thus for to liue, or not at all to liue.

NArciſſus neuer by deſire diſtreſſed,
  Elected for the ſolace of his dwelling,
The diuers coullerd Medowe liuely dreſſed,
And fed with currant freſh, of waters ſwelling.

The while he liues in libertie, thriſe bleſſed,
Loue ſees, and enuieth his life excelling,
And in the waters ſtreight, a ſhape expreſſed,
The poyſon of his life, and freedomes quelling.

So careleſſe I, that romed foorth vnarmed,
Not dreading Loue, who watches rebels narrow,
No ſooner ſawe hir eies, than inlie warmed,
With vnperceiued flames within the marrow.

And yet of both, my ſelfe moſt deepely harmed,
With waters he ? I with a burning arrow,
He drown'd in waues, the which his teares did cheriſh,
I liue in fire, and die; and yet not periſh.

THe firmament, with golden ſtars adorned,
  The Saylers watchfull eies, full well contenteth,
And afterward with tempeſt ouerſpred,
The abſent lights of heauen, he ſore lamenteth.

Your face, the firmament of my repoſe,
Long time haue kept, my waking thoughts delighted,

But now the clouds of ſorrow ouergoes
Your glorious skies,wherewith I am affrighted.

For I that haue my life and fortunes placed,
Within the ſhip,that by thoſe planets ſaileth,
By enuious chaunce,am ouermuch diſgraced,
Seeing the Loadſtar of my courſes faileth.

And yet content to drowne,without repining,
To haue my ſtars affoord the world their ſhining.

CEaſe reſtles thoughts,ſurcharg'd with heauines,
Loue,fortune,and diſdaine,with their endeuer,
The forces of my life will ſoone diſſeuer,
Without the ſting of your vnquietnes.

And thou oh hart, guiltie of my diſtreſſe,
To harbor theſe faire foes,dooſt ſtill perſeuer,
Whereby thou ſhewſt falſe traitor,thou hadſt leuer
Their conqueſt,than mine eaſe and happines.

In thee, Loues meſſengers haue taken dwelling,
Fortune in thee,hir pompe triumphant ſpreadeth,
Diſdaine hath ſpent on thee,hir bitter ſwelling,
Thus thou the root, from whence my woes proceedeth.

Ceaſe then vain thoughts,no more my ſorows double.
Loue,fortune,and diſdaine,ynough of trouble.

THinking vpon the name, by Loue engraued,
Within my hart, to be my liues directer,
The value of the whole entirely ſaued,
I reade vpon the ſillables this lecter,
Maruell,the firſt into my ſpirits ſoundeth,
And maruelling at hir,the maruell woundeth.

I

I feeke to Gaine, as by the fecond's ment,
An intereft in this admired maruaile,
But cannot finde a meane fufficient,
So hie a rated Gem to counteruaile,
  There is no weight in fire ordaind to fhine,
  Nor counterworth of any thing diuine.

The laft doth giue me counfell to Retire,
And reft content, that Loue hath bleft my fight,
And toucht my fancie with th'immortall fire,
Of this diuine, and precious Margaret,
  And thanke my fortune of exceeding fauour,
  As to be thralled to fo fweete behauiour.

O See my hart, vncertaine what effect,
  Shall finally enfue fo high a fcope,
See what it is, a Mafter to neglect,
To haue a Miftres entertaind on hope,
  He whom it was thy fortune firft to ferue,
  As fhe doth now, could neuer fee thee fterue.

There meanly lodg'd, yet mery were thy daies,
Here, high conceited intermixt with feare,
There, words and works all one, here great delaies,
There, things were in their kinde, here as they were,
  Thy hopes there fmall, but yet affured Loue,
  And here though great, God knowes if any proue.

Yet muft I not difcourage thine intent,
All paines and torments fuffred for hir fake,
May be in fine well anfwerd by euent,
If fo thy fute in time effect may take,
  But tell hir what thy former Mafter faies,
  Curfed is he that dieth through delaies.

TO make a truce, fweete Miftres with your eies,
  How often haue I proffred you my hart,
						Which

Which profers vneſteemed you deſpiſe,
As far to meane, to equall your deſart,
   Your minde wherein, all hie perfections flowe,
   Deignes not the thought, of things that are ſo lowe.

To ſtriue to alter his deſires, were vaine,
Whoſe vowed hart, affects no other place,
The which ſince you deſpiſe, I doe diſdaine,
To count it mine, as erſt before it was :
   For that is mine, which you alone alow,
   As I am yours, and onely liue for you.

Now if I him forſake, and he not finde,
His wretched exile, ſuccord by your eies,
He can not yeeld, to ſerue anothers minde,
Nor liue alone, for nature that denies,
   Then die he muſt, for other choiſe is none,
   But liue in you, or me, or die alone.

Whoſe haples death, when Fame abroad hath blowne,
Blame and reproch, procures vnto vs both,
I, as vnkinde, forſaking ſo mine owne,
But you much more, from whom the rigour groweth,
   And ſo much more, will your diſhonor be,
   By how much more, it loued you than me.

   Sweete Ladie then, the harts misfortune rue,
   Whoſe loue and ſeruice euermore was true.

SEeing thoſe eies, that with the Sun contendeth,
For maieſtie of light, and excellence,
A quickning pleaſure ſecretly deſcendeth
Into my hart, by ſubtill influence.

Not ſeeing them, horror my bliſſe depriueth,
And I, as one, by publike lawe conuicted,

                                Whom

Whom rigorouſlie, the hedſman onward driueth
To ſhamefull death, moſt heauily afflicted.

I onely liue, when I behold your ſhining,
Bright ſtars, rare lights, ſweete authors of my gladnes,
Abſent from you, my hart in ſorrow pining,
Doth feede on teares, on anguiſh, griefe, and ſadnes.

    Then maruell not, if I deſire acceſſe,
    Vnto the fountaine of my happines.

TO ſhun the death, my rare and choſen Iuell,
   That couertly, within your eies ſoiourneth,
I flie, and flying feele the fire, more cruell,
Wherewith offended, loue my ſpirits burneth.

A death moſt painfull, and the paine more bitter,
Then I returne, reſolued in opinion,
Since I muſt die, neere, or farre of, tys fitter,
To end my life, within hir eies dominion.

O then diſplaie (faire Eies) your influence,
That I, into the deeper flames aſcending,
Fall ſoone to aſhes, by hir excellence,
And better be contented with my ending.

    And all remooued, that my quiet hinders,
    Rake vp both loue, and life, within thoſe cinders.

OF all the woes my penſiue hart endureth,
   It greeues me moſt, when I my ſorrowes frame,
I knowe not what, this wretchednes procureth,
Nor whereupon I am to caſt the blame.

The fault is not in hir, for well I ſee,
I am vnworthy of hir grace, in this,

                        Nor

Nor yet in loue, who hath vouchfafed me,
To knowe within this life fo rare a bliffe.

To grieue me of my fight, then comes to minde,
As head and author of my haples woes:
But better afterward aduifde, I finde,
That onely from hir lookes, all fweetnes floes.

   And when iuft caufe of forrowing doth faile,
   I waile in fine, bicaufe I cannot waile.

DIuide my times, and rate my wretched howres,
From day to month, from month to many yeeres,
And then compare my fweeteft to my fowres,
To fee which more in equall view appeeres,
   And iudge, if for my daies and yeeres of care,
   I haue but howres of comfort to compare.

Iuft and not much, it were in thefe extreemes,
So hard a touch, and torment of the thought,
For any minde, that any right efteemes,
To yeeld fo fmall delite, fo deerely bought,
   But he that liues but in his owne defpite,
   Is not to finde his fortune by his right.

The life that ftill runs forth hir wearie waies,
With fowre to fawce the dainties of delite,
And care to choake the pleafure of hir daies,
And no rewarde, thofe many wrongs to quite,
   No blame to holde fuch irkfome time in hate,
   As but to loffe, prolongs a wretched ftate.

And fo I loath, euen to behold the light,
That fhines without all pleafure to mine eies,
With greedie wifh, I wait ftill for the night,
Yet neither this I finde, that may fuffice,

                 Not

Not that I holde, the day in more delight,
But that alike, I loath both day and night.

The day I ſee, yeelds but increaſe to care,
The night that ſhould, by nature ſerue to reſt,
Againſt hir kinde, denies ſuch eaſe to ſpare,
As pitie would affoord the ſoule oppreſt,
　　And broken ſleepes oft times preſent in ſight,
　　A dreaming wiſh, beguild with falſe delight.

The ſleepe, or elſe what ſo for ſweete appeeres,
Is vnto me but pleaſure in deſpite,
The flowre of age, the name of yonger yeeres,
Doe but vſurpe the title of delite,
　　For carefull thought, and ſorow ſundry waies,
　　Conſumes my youth, before my aged daies.

The touch, the ſting, the torment of deſire,
To ſtriue beyond the compas of reſtraint,
Kept from the reach whereto it would aſpire,
Giues cauſe (God knowes) too iuſt to my complaint,
　　Beſides the wrongs, which now with my diſtreſſe,
　　My meaning is, in ſilence to ſuppreſſe.

Oft with my ſelfe, I enter in deuice,
To reconcile theſe wearie thoughts to peace,
I treat for truce, I flatter and entice,
My wrangling wits, to worke for their releaſe,
　　But all in vaine, I ſeeke the meanes to finde,
　　That might appeaſe, the diſcord of my minde.

For when I force a fained mirth in ſhoe,
And would forget, and ſo beguile my greefe,
I cannot rid my ſelfe of ſorow ſo,
Altho I feede vpon a falſe beleeſe,
　　For inward touch of vncontented minde,
　　Returns my cares, by courſe vnto their kinde.
　　　　　　　N　　　　　　Wainde

Wainde from my will,and thus by triall taught,
How for to holde,all fortune in regard,
Though heere I boaft,a knowledge deerely bought,
Yet this poore gaine,I reape for my reward,
   I learne hereby,to harden and prepare,
   A readie minde, for all affaults of care.

Whereto,as one,euen from my cradle borne,
And not to looke for better to enfue,
I yeeld my felfe,and wifh thefe times outworne,
That but remaine,my torments to renue,
   And leaue to thofe,thefe daies of my defpite,
   Whofe better hap,may liue to more delite.

A defcription of Loue.

NOw what is Loue,I praie thee tell,
It is that fountaine and that well,
Where pleafure and repentance dwell,
It is perhaps that fauncing bell,
   That tols all in to heauen or hell,
   And this is Loue as I heare tell.

Yet what is Loue,I praie thee faie ?
It is a worke,on holie daie,
It is December matcht with Maie,
When luftie blouds in frefh araie,
   Heare ten months after of the plaie,
   And this is Loue as I heare faie.

Yet what is Loue,I praie thee faine ?
It is a Sunfhine mixt with raine,
It is a tooth ache,or like paine,
It is a game, where none doth gaine,
   The Laffe faith no,and would full faine,
   And this is Loue, as I heare faine.

                                   Yet

Yet what is Loue, I pray thee ſay,
It is a yea, it is a nay,
A pretie kinde of ſporting fray,
It is a thing will ſoone away :
    Then take the vantage while you may,
    And this is Loue, as I heare ſay.

Yet what is Loue I pray thee ſhoe,
A thing that creepes, it cannot goe,
A prize that paſſeth to and fro,
A thing for one, a thing for mo,
    And he that proues muſt finde it ſo,
    And this is Loue (ſweet friend) I troe.

The deſcription of Iealouſie.

A Seeing friend, yet enimie to reſt,
  A wrangling paſſion, yet a gladſom thought,
A bad companion, yet a welcom gueſt,
A knowledge wiſht, yet found too ſoone vnſought,
    From heauen ſuppoſde, yet ſure condemn'd to hell,
    Is Iealouſie, and there forlorne doth dwell.

And thence doth ſend fond feare and falſe ſuſpect,
To haunt our thoughts bewitched with miſtruſt,
Which breedes in vs the iſſue and effect,
Both of conceits and actions far vniuſt,
    The griefe, the ſhame, the ſmart, wherof doth proue,
    That Iealouſie's both death and hell to Loue.

For what but hell moues in the iealous hart,
Where reſtles feare works out all wanton ioyes,
Which doth both quench and kill the louing part,
And cloies the minde with worſe than knowne annoyes,
    Whoſe preſſure far exceeds hells deepe extreemes,
    Such life leads Loue entangled with miſdeemes.

Ah

AH poore Conceit, delite is dead,
    Thy pleaſant daies are doon,
The ſhadie dales muſt be his walke,
    That cannot ſee the ſunne.

The world I now to witnes call,
    The heauens my records be :
If euer I were falſe to Loue,
    Or Loue were true to me.

I knowe it now, I knew it not,
    But all too late I rew it,
I rew not that I knew it not,
    But that I euer knew it.

My care is not a fond conceit,
    That breedes a fained ſmart,
My griefes doe gripe me at the gall,
    And gnaw me at the hart.

My teares are not thoſe fained drops,
    That fall from fancies eies,
But bitter ſtreams of ſtrange diſtreſſe,
    Wherein diſcomfort lies.

My ſighes are not thoſe heauie ſighes,
    That ſhowes a ſickly breath,
My paſſions are the perfect ſignes,
    And very paines of death.

In ſum to make a dolefull end,
    To ſee my death ſo nie,
That ſorow bids me ſing my laſt,
    And ſo my ſenſes die.

SHort is my reſt, whoſe toile is ouerlong,
    My ioyes are darke, but cleere I ſee my woe,

                                          My

My ſafetie ſmall : great wracks I bide by wrong,
Whoſe time is ſwift,and yet my hap but ſloe,
    Each griefe and wound,in my poore hart appeeres,
    That laugheth howres,and weepeth many yeeres.

Deedes of the day,are fables for the night,
Sighes of deſire,are ſmoakes of thoughtfull teares,
My ſteps are falſe,although my paths be right,
Diſgrace is bolde,and fauor full of feares,
    Diſquiet ſleepe, keepes audit of my life,
    Where rare content,doth make diſpleaſure rife.

The dolefull bell,that is the voice of time,
Cals on my end, before my haps be ſeene,
Thus fals my hopes,whoſe harmes haue power to clime,
Not come to haue that long in wiſh hath beene,
    I ſeeke your loue,and feare not others hate,
    Be you with me,and I haue Cæſars ſtate.

The praiſe of Virginitie.

Virginitie reſembleth right the Roſe,
    That gallantly within the garden growes,
    Whilſt in the mothers bodie it doth ſtand,
Of nibling ſheep vntoucht,or ſhepherds hand.
The aire thereon,and ruddie morne doth ſmile,
The earth and waters,fauours it that while,
Braue luſtie youth,and the inamord Dame,
Euen ſo doth age,and temples craue the ſame.

But when from naturall ſtalke, it is remou'd,
And place where it,ſo highly was belou'd,
The grace that earth,and heauen thereon did caſt,
With beautie,fauor,loue, and all, is paſt.
                    Euen

Euen ſo the Maid, when once hir flowre is loſt,
More deere than eie, or life, or what is moſt,
The loue and liking which ſhe had before,
Forgoeth quite, and ſhe eſteem'd no more.

    Ladies Lenuoy to you that haue this prize,
    I reed ye hold your owne, if you be wiſe.

O Night, O ielious night, repugnant to my pleaſures,
  O night ſo long deſir'd, yet croſſe to my content,
Ther's none but onely thou that can performe my pleaſures,
Yet none but onely thou that hindereth my intent.

Thy beams, thy ſpiteful beams, thy lamps that burn to brightly,
Diſcouer all my traines, and naked lay my dtifts,
That night by night I hope, yet faile my purpoſe nightly,
Thy enuious glaring gleame defeateth ſo my ſhifts.

Sweet night withhold thy beams, withhold them til to morow,
Whoſe ioyes in lack ſo long, a hell of torments breedes,
Sweete night, ſweete gentle night, doe not prolong my ſorow,
Deſire is guide to me, and Loue no Loadſtar needes.

Let Sailers gaze on ſtars and Moone ſo freſhly ſhining,
Let them that miſſe the way be guided by the light,
I knowe my Ladies bowre, there needes no more diuining,
Affection ſees in darke, and Loue hath eies by night.

Dame Cinthia couch awhile, holde in thy hornes for ſhining,
And glad not lowring night, with thy too glorious raies,
But be ſhe dim and darke, tempeſtuous and repining,
That in hir ſpite, my ſport may worke thy endles praiſe.

And when my will is wrought, then Cinthia ſhine good Ladie,
All other nights and daies, in honour of that night,
That happie heauenly night, that night ſo darke and ſhadie,
Wherein my Loue had eies, that lighted my delight.

                         Sweete

SWeete Violets (Loues paradice) that ſpred
    Your gracious odours, which you couched beare,
      Within your palie faces,
Vpon the gentle wing of ſome calme breathing winde,
    That plaies amidſt the plaine,
    If by the fauour of propicious ſtars you gaine,
Such grace as in my Ladies boſome place to finde,
    Be prowd to touch thoſe places,
    And whē hir warmth your moiſture forth doth wear,
Whereby hir daintie parts are ſweetly fed,
      Your honors of the flowrie meads I pray,
      You pretie daughters of the earth and Sun,
      With milde and ſeemly breathing ſtraight diſplay,
      My bitter ſighes that haue my hart vndoon.

Vermilion Roſes that with new daies riſe,
    Diſplay your Crimſen folds freſh looking faire,
      Whoſe radiant bright, diſgraces
The rich adorned raies of Roſeat riſing morne,
    (Ah) if hir virgins hand
    Doe pluck your pure, ere Phœbus view the land,
And vaile your gracious pomp in louely natures ſcorne,
    If chaunce my Miſtres traces,
    Faſt by your flowres to take the Sommers aire,
Then wofull bluſhing tempt hir glorious eies,
      To ſpread their teares Adonis death reporting,
      And tell Loues torments ſorowing for hir frend,
      Whoſe drops of blood within your leaus côſorting
      Report faire Venus mones withouten end.

    Then may remorſe (in pitying of my ſmart)
    Drie vp my teares, and dwell within hir hart.

AVrora now, began to riſe againe,
  From watrie couch, and from old Tithons ſide,
In hope to kiſſe vpon Acteian plaine,
Yong Cephalus, and through the golden glide,

                    On

On Eaſterne coaſt,ſhe caſt ſo great a light,
That Phœbus thought it time to make retire,
From Thetis Bowre,wherein he ſpent the night,
To light the world againe with heauenly fire.

Nor ſooner gan his winged ſteedes to chaſe,
The Stigian night,mantled with duskie vale,
But poore Amyntas,haſteth him apace,
In deſarts thus, to weepe a wofull tale.

Now ſilent ſhades,and all that dwell therein,
As Birds,or Beaſts, or Wormes that creepe on grounde,
Diſpoſe your ſelues to teares,while I begin,
To rew the griefe, of mine eternall wounde.

And dolefull ghoſts,whoſe nature flies the light,
Come ſeate your ſelues with me on eu'ry ſide,
And whilſt I die for want of my delight,
Lament the woes that Fancie me betide.

Phillis is dead,the marke of my deſire,
My cauſe of loue,and ſhipwracke of my ioyes,
Phillis is gone,that ſet my hart on fire,
That clad my thoughts with ruinous annoyes.

Phillis is fled,and bides I wot not where,
Phillis(alas)the praiſe of woman kinde,
Phillis the Sun of this our hemiſphere,
Whoſe beames made me and many others blinde.

But blinded me (poore man)aboue the reſt,
That like olde Oedipus, I liue in thrall,
Still feele the worſt, and neuer hope the beſt,
My mirth in mone,my honie drownd in gall.

Hir faire,but cruell eies,bewitcht my ſight,
Hir ſweete,but fading ſpeech,enthrald my thought,

                      And

And in hir deeds,I reaped ſuch delight,
As brought both will,and libertie to nought.

Therefore all hope of happines adue,
Adue deſire the ſource of all my care,
Diſpaire me tels my weale will nere renue,
Till this my ſoule,doth paſſe in Charons Crare.

Meane time my minde muſt ſuffer Fortunes skorne,
My thoughts ſtil wound,like wounds that ſtil are green
My weakned lyms,be laide on beds of thorne,
My life decaies,although my death foreſeene.

Mine eies,now eies no more,but ſeas of teares,
Weepe on your fill,to coole my burning breſt,
Where Loue did place deſire,twixt hope,and feares,
(I ſaie)deſire,the author of vnreſt.

And (would to gods)Phillis where ere thou be,
Thy ſoule did ſee,the ſowre of mine eſtate,
My ioyes eclipſt,for onely want of thee,
My being with my ſelfe at foule debate.

My humble vowes,my ſufferance of woe,
My ſobs,and ſighes,my euerwatching eies,
My plaintife teares,my wandring to and froe,
My will to die,my neuer ceaſing cries.

No doubt but then,thy ſorrows would perſwade,
The doome of death,to cut my vitall twiſt,
That I with thee,amidſt th'infernall ſhade,
And thou with me,might ſport vs as we liſt.

O if thou waite on faire Proſerpines traine,
And heareſt Orpheus,neere th'Eliſian ſprings,
Entreat thy Queene,to free thee thence againe,
And let the Thracian guide thee with his ſtrings.

     T. W. Gent.

    O   Away

A Way diſpaire, the death of hopeles harts,
For hope and truth, aſſure me long agoe,
That pleaſure is the end of lingring ſmarts,
When time, with iuſt content, rewardeth woe.

Sweete vertues throne is built in labours towre,
Where Lawrell wreath's are twiſt for them alone,
Whoſe gals are burſt with often taſte of ſowre,
Whoſe blis from bale is ſprong, whoſe mirth frō mone.

I therefore ſtriue by toyles, to raiſe my name,
And Iaſon like, to gaine a golden fleece,
The end of eu'ry worke doth crowne the ſame,
As witnes well, the happie harmes of Greece :
    For if the Greekes, had ſoone got Pryams ſeat,
    The glory of their paines, had not been great.

T. W. Gent.

I Hope and feare, that for my weale or woe,
That heau'nly lampe, which yeelds both heat & light,
To make a throne, for gods on earth belowe,
Is cut in twaine, and fixt in my delight,
    Which two faire hemyſpheres, through light & heat,
    Planting deſire, driue reaſon from hir ſeate.

No, no, my too forgetfull toong blaſpheames,
I ſhould haue ſaide, that where theſe hemiſpheres,
In harts, through eies, fixe hot and lightſome beames,
There reaſon works deſire, and hopes breed feares,
    O onely obieƈt, for an Eagles eie,
    Whoſe light, and heate, make men to liue and die.

Twixt theſe, a daintie paradiſe doth lie,
As ſweete as in the Sunne the Phenix Bowre,
As white as ſnowe, as ſmooth as Iuorie,

As

As faire, as Pſyches boſome, in that howre,
    When ſhe diſcloſde the boxe of Beauties Queene,
    All this and more, is in Sibilla ſeene.
                 T. W. Gent.

SIr painter, are thy colours redie ſet,
    My Miſtreſſe can not be with thee to day,
    Shee's gone into the field to gather May,
The timely Prymroſe, and the Violet :
    Yet that thou maiſt, not diſapointed bee,
    Come draw hir picture by my fantaſee.

And well for thee, to paint hir by thine eare,
    For ſhould thine eie, vnto that office ſerue,
    Thine Eie, and Hand, thy Art, & Hart, would ſwerue,
Such maieſtie hir countenance doth beare,
    And where thou wert Apelles thought before,
    For failing ſo, thou ſhouldſt be praiſd no more.

Drawe firſt hir Front, a perfect Iuorie white,
    Hie, ſpatious, round, and ſmooth on either ſide,
    Hir temples brancht with vains, blew, opening wide.
As in the Map, Danubius runs in ſight :
    Colour hir ſemicircled browes with iet,
    The throne where Loue triumphantly doth ſet.

Regard hir Eie, hir eie, a woondrous part,
    It woundeth deepe, and cureth by and by,
    It driues away, and draweth curteouſly,
It breeds and calmes, the tempeſt of the hart,
    And what to lightning Ioue, belongeth too,
    The ſame hir lookes, with more effect can doe.

Hir Cheeke, reſembleth euerie kinde of way,
    The Lillie ſtainde, with ſweete Adonis blood,
    As wounded he ſtrai'd vp and downe the wood,
For whome faire Venus languiſht many a day,
            O 2   Or

Or plainly more to anſwere your demaune,
Hir cheekes are Roſes, ouercaſt with lawne.

Hir louely Lip, doth others all excell,
On whom it pleaſe (ay me) a kiſſe beſtoe,
He neuer taſteth afterward of woe,
Such ſpeciall vertue in the toutch doth dwell :
    The colour tempred of the morning red,
    Wherewith Aurora doth adorne hir head.

Hir ample Cheſt, an heauenly plot of ground,
The ſpace betweene, a Paradiſe at leaſt,
Parnaſſus like, hir twifolde mounting breaſt,
Hir heauenly graces, heapingly abound,
    Loue ſpreads his conquering colours in this feeld,
    Whereto the race of Gods and men doe yeeld.

The other parts, which cuſtom doth conceale,
Within a ſarcenet vaile thou muſt conuay,
So due proportion well diſcerne I may,
What though the garment doe not all reueale,
    The ſhadow of a naked thigh may fraight,
    His head brim full, hath any fine conceit.

Before hir Feete, vpon a Marble ſtone,
Inflamed with the Sunbeames of hir eie,
Depaint my hart that burneth paſſionately,
And if thy penſill can ſet downe ſuch mone,
    Thy picture ſelfe, will teeling ſemblance make,
    Of ruthe and pitie for my torments ſake.

How now Apelles, are thy ſenſes tane ?
Haſt drawne a picture, or drawne out thy hart ?
Wilt thou be held a Maſter of thine art,
And temper colours tending to thy bane ?
    Happie my hart, that in hir Sunſhine fries,
    Aboue thy hap that in hir ſhadow dies.

I

I Pray thee Loue, ſay, whither is this poſting,
Since with thy deitie firſt I was acquainted,
I neuer ſaw thee thus diſtraƈted coaſting,
    With countenance tainted.

Thy conquering arrowes broken in thy quiuer,
Thy brands that woont the inward marrow ſunder,
Fireles and forceles, all a peeces ſhiuer,
    With mickle wonder.

That maketh next my ſtayleſſe thoughts to houer,
I cannot ſound this vncouth cauſe of beeing,
The vaile is torne that did thy viſage couer,
    And thou art ſeeing.

A ſtranger, one (quoth Loue) of good demerit,
Did ſute and ſeruice to his Soueraine proffer,
In any caſe ſhe would not ſeeme to heare it,
    But ſcornd the offer.

And very now vpon this Maying morrow,
By breake of day, he found me at my harbour,
I went with him, to vnderſtand his ſorrow,
    Vnto hir Arbour.

Where he Loue torments dolefully vnfolded,
With words, that might a Tigers hart haue charmed,
His ſighes and teares, the mountaine yee had moulted,
    And ſhe not warmed.

Hir great diſdaine againſt hir Louer proued,
Kindled my brand, that to hir breſt I ſeated,
The flame betweene hir paps, them often moued.
    Nor burnt, nor heated.

My arrowes keene I afterward aſſaied,
Which from hir breſt without effeƈt rebounded.
       And

And as a ball, on Marble floore they plaied,
         With force confounded.

The brand that burnt, old Pryams Towne to aſshes,
Now firſt his operation, wants it than,
The darts that Emerald skies in peeces daſshes,
         Skornd by a woman.

Thus while I ſaide, ſhe toward me arriued,
And with a tutch of triumph, neuer doubted,
To teare the vaile, that vſe of ſight bereaued,
         So Loue was louted.

The vaile of error, from mine eies bereaued,
I ſawe heauens hope, and earth hir treaſurie,
Well maiſt thou erre ſaid I, I am deceiued,
         Bent to pleaſure thee.

Ceaſe haples man, my ſuccors to importune,
Shee onely ſhee, my ſtratagemes repelleth,
Vainly endeuor I, to tempt hir Fortune,
         That ſo excelleth.

Content thee man, that thou didſt ſee and ſuffer,
And be content, to ſuffer, ſee, and die,
And die content, bicauſe thou once didſt mooue hir,
         She diſpleaſd thereby.

And herewithall I left the man a dyeng,
For by his paſſions I perceiu'd none other,
I hie me thus aſham'd with ſpeedie flyeng,
         To tell my Mother.

F I N I S.